IRREGULAR PEOPLE

JOYCE LANDORF
HEATHERLEY

IRREGULAR PEOPLE

BALCONY PUBLISHING

AUSTIN, TEXAS 78734

Library of Congress Cataloging in Publication Data:

Heatherley, Joyce Landorf
Irregular people.

Bibliography: p. 157.
1. Interpersonal relations. 2. Christian life—
1900-   . 3. Spiritual healing. 4. Landorf,
Joyce. 1. Title.
HM132.L348 1982   302.3'4   82-50842
ISBN 0-929488-00-8

Scripture quotations in this publication are from the following sources:

The King James Version of the Bible (KJV).

The Living Bible; Paraphrased (TLB), copyright © 1971 by
Tyndale House Publishers, Wheaton, Illinois.

The Revised Standard Version of the Bible (RSV), copyright 1946,
1952 © 1971 and 1973 by the Division of Christian Education
of the National Council of Churches of Christ in the U.S.A.

The Modern Language Bible: The New Berkeley Version in Modern English,
copyright © 1945, 1959, 1969 by Zondervan Publishing House.

The New Testament in Modern English,
copyright © 1958, 1959, 1960 by J. B. Phillips, used by
permission of the Macmillan Company.

PRINTED IN THE UNITED STATES OF AMERICA

Joyce Landorf Heatherley

Dear Special Person,

The subject of "Irregular People" has been quietly simmering on the back burner of my mind for half a dozen years. For the last two years, it's been scalding my soul. Now the temperature is rising, and I must write.

How do I begin? How dare I write about the troubled waters of our lives? Especially when in some cases, like mine, the waters not only are troubled; they are boiling, and I feel like I'm drowning in them.

Fifteen years have gone by since my best friend, my mother, died. Now, as I look back, I see clearly that for most of these intervening years I have had to face, cope with, and deal with two common yet emotionally formidable burdens.

On one hand, I experienced the immediate and devastating sense of grief and loss. Yet out of that bereavement came the book, *Mourning Song,* and I praise the Lord for taking my utter despair and, from it, creating something so healing. It was as if God, through that writing, confirmed what He wrote through Paul about the "whys" of suffering: "Blessed be the God and Father of our Lord Jesus Christ, the Father of mercies and God of all comfort, who comforts us in all our affliction, so that we may be able to comfort those who are in any affliction, with the comfort with which we ourselves are comforted by God" (2 Cor. 1:3–4, RSV). For I was able to pass on the same comfort God had given me in my painful loss.

On the other hand, my mother's death produced a sharpening of focus in another area. Gradually I was made

5

acutely aware of a complicated relationship within our family. It was an unseen, gnawing type of enigma which, while my mother was alive, had stayed submerged and fairly well below the surface.

Recently, as I watched the magnificent actress, Katherine Hepburn, play the part of a wife and mother in the movie, *On Golden Pond,* I caught a glimpse of my own growing-up years. As the story unfolded, I realized that my own mother had behaved and spoken in many of the same ways.

I loved the moment when Miss Hepburn tells her amusing but acerbic and pessimistic husband (played by Henry Fonda) that their daughter is coming to visit them, and then gently puts the question to him, "Wouldn't it be nice if we could all get along this time?"

I wondered how many mothers or fathers or brothers or sisters all over the world have verbalized the very same question just before some holiday or family reunion.

When my own mother died, the number-one catalyst for smoothing out painful relationships in my family left us, and the bonds of our love were stretched with a new kind of suffering.

About eight years after her death, the true nature of this painful relationship came to a head during a family dispute—much like an ugly, red, swollen boil. I knew then that only a lancing of the wound would ever produce a healing. I remember that, at the time of this terrible confrontation, I felt I would surely die of the infection of bitterness, but the God who loves you and me and has "planned out our days," as David tells us in Psalm 139, caused two things to happen at that point.

One, a friend wrote me a letter which God used as a scalpel to open the infectious boil, and the first of many, many healings began to repair my soul and spirit.

Two, I began to realize that even in Christian families it is *not* uncommon to endure immense suffering from a destructive relationship with a mother, father, brother, sister, husband, wife, or in-law.

One of the *Los Angeles Times* staff writers, James Brown, recently wrote a review about the TV show, "Eight Is Enough." [1] He compared it to the classic, "Father Knows Best," and pointed out that in television writing we just *know* each conflict will work out just fine.

It seems to me that screenwriters, like all writers, feel safer *not* exposing themselves to write about frustrating and difficult emotions which are formed from family conflicts. Besides, what authors love to do is give *solutions*. We hate to admit to frustration which often ends in futile exasperation.

Brown ends his review by saying of television writing, "Most of the time, crisis is resolved in a neatly wrapped package where everybody learns, everybody grows, and nobody's late for dinner."

In this book, it's my prayer that everybody learns and everybody grows. But the problems of family relationships are so complex; I certainly do not want to write "x"-number of pages of neatly wrapped up, pat answers. Also, I'm certain *someone* will always be late for dinner!

It's one thing for any author to write in a detached, generalized, and clinical way about people and relationships, and quite another to write about personal, complicated relationships within one's own family. So I've been torn, for months now, between *knowing* I must write on this grievous subject and daily *procrastinating* the moment of exposing my heart.

I grew up in a home where my parents always had a "promise box" to which we could turn in times of special need. And since my whole family and I have been Christians, we have had a series of promise boxes. We seem to have lost a couple of them to moving vans, but the one we have now is shaped like a loaf of bread, and the paper cards still come in the summer-faded colors. It features the traditional printing—a Scripture verse on one side and four lines of a hymn or poem on the other. And there is something very warm that stirs my memories each time I reach into this miniature warehouse of God's promises.

Just a few days ago I told my daughter, Laurie, and my daughter-by-love, Teresa, that I was having an awful time actually getting started writing about irregular people. We discussed various beginning paragraphs, but all of us ended up shrugging our shoulders. I was still idea-less a few days later when I pulled out a promise from the box on my shelf.

Now, while I don't believe in "Lady Luck," good or bad fortune, or coincidences, I still had to sit down a moment, after I read the Scripture side of the promise, to marvel at God's ability to reach down and touch the point of our greatest need with His *Word!*

On the first line of the card, Jeremiah, that great patriarch of the faith, said, "Ah, Lord God! behold, I cannot...." (Jer. 1:6, KJV). I thought to myself, that's exactly where I am with this book. I cannot! I plainly and simply cannot. I cannot write this book about those disturbing family relationships which involve such crucial problems, to name a few, as accepting rejection, understanding abandonment, and living with verbal or nonverbal abuse. I cannot show anyone my scars. I cannot deal with the problems of handling difficult people—irregular people—especially when often it means coping in this Christian life with relatives who can be everything from "a little difficult to get along with" to utterly crushing. I cannot. I cannot!

Then I read the second line on the card. It was not God's immediate answer to Jeremiah, but one found later in the thirty-second chapter. The Lord identified Himself with, "Behold, I am the Lord, the God of all flesh." Then He merely asked the question, "Is there any thing too hard for me?" (v. 27, KJV).

I had to smile. Even the color of that little card was green. Green for "go." The signal light had turned green, and with those verses tucked away tightly inside my heart and mind, the courage to write began to build.

First, though, I wanted to know a little more about a man of God who had the nerve to say to the Lord with such honesty, "I cannot!" I found Ray Stedman's book, *Expository Studies in Jeremiah*, [2] on my shelf, and I've been reading and studying Jeremiah ever since.

8

What a man Jeremiah was! How refreshing his open, transparent honesty, how beautiful his indefatigable courage, and how astonishing that he was not controlled by his awful circumstances.

I read the full text of Jeremiah, chapter one, and unabashedly it reads, " 'O Lord God' I said, 'I can't do that! I'm far too young! I'm only a youth!' " (v. 6). Actually, the prophet was around thirty, but in those days nobody listened to you unless you were a matured ninety-year-old.

However, listen to the Lord's answer: " 'Don't say that,' he replied, 'for you will go wherever I send you and speak whatever I tell you to. And don't be afraid of the people, for I, the Lord, will be with you and see you through' " (vv. 7–8, TLB).

Another translation ends that portion of the verse with the words, "Never fear their faces, for I am with you to rescue you, says the Lord" (v. 8, MLB).

Just recently I spoke to an outdoor crowd of over seven thousand people at the "Jesus Northwest Festival" held at the Vancouver, Washington fairgrounds. The people were spread out before me on the hillsides, threatening rain clouds edged closer to the bandshell where I was standing, and the wind whipped up a piercing gale. To top it all off, I'd been asked to speak on "Irregular People," so I did—but never with more reluctance. When I finished (fortunately, ahead of the rain), I stumbled off towards backstage and made my way to a more private place.

I wondered aloud why I always felt so vulnerable and naked when I stood on a platform speaking to audiences about irregular people. I think it has a lot to do with the seriousness of the subject. Difficult and yes, even impossible, relationships create some of the most dysfunctional family situations in the world. That day I felt the intense need for the healing of our memories in relationships—a need that cuts across all social and cultural levels.

I left the fairgrounds that Saturday totally drained in spirit and in health, but I fervently prayed that the Lord had used my words on that cloudy, windy day to heal troubled hearts.

The next morning I had to speak at People's Church of Salem, Oregon, and after the services a young couple drove us to Portland so we could catch the plane home. On the way to the hotel and airport, our driver shared this story.

He had heard me speak before and had enjoyed my talk, but he was an outdoorsman, an expert fisherman, and, frankly, had *not* wanted to waste a perfectly good Saturday afternoon at the fairgrounds to hear me. However, his wife had insisted, and so with an unwilling spirit he had come and begun to hear about irregular people.

"For the first ten minutes or so, I kept wondering why I had agreed to come," he said. "I was getting nothing out of what you were saying. As far as I could tell, I did not have anyone in my life who was 'irregular' to me. Then, when you were about fifteen or twenty minutes into your talk, I realized with a shock that I *did* have a person exactly like you were describing."

The young man was shaking his head in disbelief, and he continued by saying, "It dawned on me that my person is my father, and he has been irregular to me all my life! As you talked, piece after piece of a puzzle began to fit together . . . questions, attitudes, my reactions, my father's words. They all began to make sense. By the time you were finished, I wanted to run up there on that stage and hug you. God used everything you said to really hit home, and there was real healing for my life yesterday afternoon."

His story was just the first of many verifications from the Lord that, though this book is definitely a painful disclosure and one that makes me extremely vulnerable, I must write it down.

It's true—the waters are very hot and I still "cannot," but the Lord's promise is before me. " 'I am with you to rescue . . . you,' says the Lord." I can do "all things," not by my strength or by my power, but by God's Spirit!

This still well may be the most difficult and demanding book of my life. My heart is tender and to the breaking point. These pages will undoubtedly produce deep soul-searching. Writing this will be a scalding-yet-soothing, a painful-yet-healing, a difficult-yet-necessary, and a breaking-yet-mending experience.

Is there something you cannot do, cannot say, cannot fix, cannot reconcile, cannot feel, cannot give, or cannot heal? I'm sure there is. But take heart and a measureful of hope from old Jeremiah—the "cannots" of our lives are the very vehicles for God's "can-dos." There is nothing too hard for Him.

The Lord will see us through. And, though the waters are troubled and very hot, we will not drown.

He and He alone is able.

In His love,

Joyce

Joyce Landorf Heatherley

CHAPTER ONE

THE INTERVIEW WAS OVER. I watched the young Diane-Keaton look-alike as she wrapped up her radio talk show with an adroit assessment of my book, *Joseph*. She was, and is, reputed to be one of the hottest names in radio, and though she's young she's already won several prestigious awards. She is also Jewish, bright, and *very* articulate.

I loved the interview. Her sharp, penetrating questions and her complete grasp of Joseph's character told me that she, unlike many Christian broadcasters, had actually read *Joseph* from cover to cover. I was impressed!

After she had given a final nod to the engineer, she picked up her notes and asked, more out of politeness than anything else, "Now that *Joseph* is out, I suppose you'll be doing another book . . ."

I nodded yes.

"On what?" she asked casually.

"On your irregular person."

"Irregular?" She looked at me quizzically.

"Yes, that person in your life who really bugs you to death."

She digested that for a split second, and then dismissed it as an unimportant book by saying, "But don't you think life is full of those irregular kinds of people? There's this guy here at the station . . ." she gestured with her hands, and I understood. "There's the clerk in some store, or the freeway driver. They all bug us to death. We are surrounded by that kind of person . . ." Her voice trailed off and implied that she didn't think I'd have a whole lot to say about irregular people, because we are simply living in a world where we are stuck with them. The look in her very pert, brown eyes also suggested that she was wondering why anybody would take the time and energy to bother with what was merely a fact of life.

"That's not exactly who I mean," I volunteered. "The irregular person I'm talking about is a person you are related to—like your parents, a brother, sister, cousin, uncle, aunt, or even in-laws. And, in some cases, even a husband or a wife."

Abruptly she stopped shuffling papers, leaned across the table, and said intently, "I see. Well, let me tell you, when that book is out, *please* come back for an interview—*nobody ever* talks about *that* person!"

Then, even though both our day's schedules were already frantically jammed, we stayed for another half-hour and talked about her person.

Most everyone has at least one person in their life who truly makes living one continuous pain in the derrière. What heightens the pain is that this person is not a mere acquaintance of ours. No, unfortunately it is more complicated than that, for we are related to them, either by birth or marriage.

Some of you may not have any relative who regularly rains on your life's parade, but others—and you have my undying and sympathetic support—are blessed with not one, but two or three such persons.

However, as I told the young woman at the radio station, it is important to explain who I am *not* talking about before we move on.

I'm certainly not referring to the countless number of human beings who cross our paths in our jobs, our neighborhoods, our stores, our towns, or on our highways and

14

byways. I'm not even talking about those who intermittently and temporarily irritate and exasperate us, who occasionally frustrate our lives and play havoc with our frazzled emotions. Those people are transient, and they weave in and out of our lives on a very limited basis. They are best known for the moments when they give us a short, limited pain in our necks. Here are some examples of the kind of person who bugs us in a limited way:

—The arrogant man who parks in the space for the handicapped at the shopping center, because the laws and rules were made for other people to obey.

—The older lady at the airport who pushes herself in front of you and eighty-nine others as you wait for your seat assignments and boarding passes.

—The inconsiderate driver who weaves in and out of traffic, jeopardizing his (and everyone else's) safety.

—The teacher or professor who regularly and almost gleefully points out your total of incorrect answers while adroitly assassinating your character and personhood.

—The insensitive pastor who tells you to "cheer up, because things could be worse," right after you've told him your life is the pits.

—The people who call themselves your friends but who rarely ever say an encouraging word to you.

You could probably add to my list of temporarily irregular people, but all of these people have this one thing in common: your relationship with them can be terminated in one way or another. You have a choice.

—You can call the police on the illegally parked person, make a citizen's arrest, or go do your shopping.

—You can be as rude as the old lady at the airport, and push her out of line. Or you can stand there, tuck the experience into the back burner of your mind, and remember it so you won't do that when you're her age.

—You can watch for that wild and crazy driver the next

time you travel that route, or you can accept the fact that you may never see that particular offender again, and see to it that you drive safely *and* defensively.

—You can be transferred to another class with a different teacher, or better yet, you can graduate from that school and get away from the whole mess.

—You can have a confrontation with your pastor, seek out another more spiritually mature pastor, or you can even begin the search for a new church.

—As to your friends, you can *lovingly* confront them with the conflict, acknowledging where you two stand, or you can simply stop inviting them to lunch, stop sending birthday presents, and terminate the relationship.

I'm certainly not suggesting here that these alternatives offer any instant cures. There are no painless answers that will magically unravel life's knots. But, the point is, there are several alternatives open in dealing with people who temporarily and only occasionally interrupt the flow of our lives. Not so with those who are related to us. They are a permanent part of our lives.

Holidays, birthdays, funerals, the birth or christening of a baby, weddings, showers, and family reunions all bring home the fact that coping and accepting the irregular person or persons in our lives is one of the most exasperating tasks of our existence. As a friend put it, "Holidays . . . what are they? *Pain* and to be dreaded!"

While I don't have specific documentation, I am convinced that one of the major contributing factors for the high suicide rate immediately after the Christmas holidays is because families have been "together." Once more, new wounds are made, old ones are opened up, and the scars continue to remain unhealed.

As a friend declared in January of this year, "Well, this past Christmas *both* my wife's parents and mine came to our house for dinner. . . . The remarkable thing is that we are still a family. Our children came through, our marriage held together, and somehow we all survived another 'happy holiday' . . . but just barely."

If you are one of those rare people who do not have such an irregular person, then thank the Lord this moment. You are like angels' visits—few and far between. But even if you don't relate to what I'm writing at this moment, please continue to read. There is always the possibility that you, without knowing it, are someone else's irregular person. And while *you* might not have an irregular person, I can guarantee you that *someone* in your family *does*—and for their sake, if not yours, you need to become aware of this almost invisible closet problem. Who knows? Maybe you will be the heaven-sent person in your family to bring about a much-needed, long-sought-after reconciliation between various members of your family.

Or perhaps you will be like the woman who, due to being recently graduated from college with big bills and small income, was financially unable to attend a day-long seminar of mine. When a generous friend paid her way, she told me later she felt excited in going, because she knew God had something very special for her to learn.

The young woman had a delayed reaction to the seminar, especially to "Irregular People," as I spoke on this topic that day. Six months later she wrote:

> On that Saturday, I was very impressed with your statement, "God doesn't make mistakes." It really helped me to give up some feelings as God wanted me to. However, at the time, I really didn't see how the main thrust of your message applied to me.
>
> You spoke that afternoon about dealing with people (mostly relatives) with whom we just don't get along. I didn't see that I *had* any of those people in my life.
>
> It wasn't until a month or so later that I realized God had been preparing me for just that sort of conflict.
>
> Always, in the past, I'd assumed total guilt for a certain

relationship and in a particular situation, even though I didn't see a logical reason to do so.

Now, I see, we are two people. We don't *have* to agree. Also, I've finally been able to commit the situation to God. The Lord is making such a difference in my life. It just hit me that this wonderful change in my Christian life began with that seminar that God brought me to so wonderfully, and with a message I didn't really understand at the time.

I just wanted you to know how the Lord used you to help me, so that you might share in my praise to Him!

I admit that for a number of years I didn't think anyone but me had experienced this kind of complicated and painful relationship with a person in their family. Then, at the height of my frustration, when I was filled with anger and feelings of guilt, I began whispering a question to a few close friends, "Do you have anyone in your family who truly bugs you?"

Very quickly, from all sorts of friends and family, the response was whispered back: *"Yes! I do! You, too?"*

I also never knew what to call my person. Because, as I have already said, my intention in lecturing or writing about this person was *not* to hurt or embarrass anyone. Each time I referred to him, I desperately needed a method of identification. I didn't know what to call anyone's person, much less mine, until I saw a television movie.

This story, written by Bette Greene in her award-winning book (which I read long after I'd seen the film) was entitled *Summer of My German Soldier*. It was the author's own story, and the events portrayed occurred in the early 1940s.[1]

Since I was only about ten years old at the time of the Second World War, I was unaware of the fact that small groups of German soldiers were brought to several southern states and put into internment camps. This forcefully written movie concerns itself with one of those groups who were brought to a small town in Arkansas. The drama cen-

18

ters around a young German prisoner who escapes and is accidentally discovered by a twelve-year-old girl named Patty Bergen. She is the daughter of a Jewish couple who own the local dry goods store.

Patty befriends the boy and hides him in a small playroom above her father's unused barn. She tells no one that he is there.

As the days go on, a friendship/love relationship begins to develop between the two young people, even though they are from very different worlds. Patty is newly awakened to the almost unbelievable thought that somebody in this world of hers really thinks she's valuable. Somebody acts as if he actually likes her as a person! You become aware, as the story unfolds, that perhaps she has never been given or ever had parental approval or acceptance.

The film depicts Patty's mother as being somewhat insipid, like a lukewarm cup of tea. She seems to have no opinions or direction in her life, and the only affection she shows is directed at Patty's younger sister, Sharon. The mother seems to be neither strong nor weak—she just appears to have lost the lemon and sugar of her life.

But the father is depicted in quite another way. He is a kaleidoscope of conflicting emotions—hot, freezing, and then back to warm, even loving. Unlike most television portrayals which paint their characters *all* black or *all* white, this film gives the father many shades of gray. Sometimes Patty's father is with her on an issue—he's loyal and supportive. Other times he seems completely insensitive to her needs. Occasionally, he is given to beating her with his belt. For a while, I couldn't decide whether he was a hero or a villain, and since that is so true of people in real life, I found the character portrait simply fascinating.

At the same time, though, I was beginning to experience some emotional discomfort of my own, because I know people *do* have parents like this. I know of many people who are not *all* bad, but at times—especially when their acceptance is needed the most—they simply become invisible, or their reaction to a situation is very abnormal or wildly bizarre. So I began to really listen for whatever message this TV movie had to offer.

Near the end of the story, the German boy realizes that the F.B.I. is getting very close to discovering his hideout at Patty's home. So he leaves one night in the hope that she will not be implicated or brought up on charges for harboring a prisoner of war. But as he is fleeing for his life, the F.B.I. catches up with him and kills him.

Earlier in the story, Patty has given the boy her father's monogrammed shirt to wear instead of his prison shirt. It is this same white shirt, now torn and bloodied by a bullet wound, that the F.B.I. traces, in the early hours of the morning, to the Bergen house.

The film's scene that begins to take hold of the jugular vein opens as Mr. and Mrs. Bergen and the F.B.I. agents come into Patty's bedroom. She is awakened from a sound sleep by an agent who throws the boy's bloodied shirt on her bed and begins questioning her.

Instantly Patty's face registers the whole story. She knows now that he is dead. The shirt with the bullet hole and the blood is in front of her, and it's definitely the one she gave him.

Patty goes into shock. Her father comes unglued. He is not about to believe that his daughter could be a part of this. Yet the evidence is crushingly overwhelming. He begins to realize she is guilty but, while the F.B.I. agents are there, he controls his emotions.

On the following day, however, Patty stays in her room, refusing to come downstairs. And the scene that will remain very clear in my soul for a long time to come begins to unfold.

Patty's father comes into her bedroom and makes some genial small talk. He tells her that it would be polite for her to let her mother know if she's coming downstairs for lunch or not, and then he begins to verbalize what he has really come upstairs to say.

He tells her that he has already spoken with a lawyer who will represent her if there is a trial. But at the same time he gives her some bit of assurance by telling her that the attorney doesn't believe she is *"legally"* a traitor.

Patty doesn't say anything during this time. She just continues to rock in her chair. Then, very abruptly, her father turns toward her, and his whole face becomes a contorted mass of fury. He directs a mounting tirade of words to his daughter in a voice choked by hatred. Michael Constantine, the actor who played the part of the father, gave a superb and convincing performance as he proceeded to annihilate his daughter with a polluted stream of verbal abuse.

He goes back in his memory to when Patty was born, and describes it as the saddest day of his life. And then he recalls his own relationship with his mother—and how she had "plenty of love" for his father and brothers, but not any for him. He tells Patty that she looks just like his mother, and that the resemblance showed even through the glass window in the nursery when Patty was born. He goes on to tantalize her with something she never knew about when he drops the hint that he and her mother wouldn't even have *had* to get married if it hadn't been for her.

Patty has stopped rocking by now, and she stares up at her father, trying to comprehend all that he is spewing out on her. And then he snarls, "I knew right away when I saw you in the nursery that you hated me . . . but I never, not in all my dreams, thought you'd go this far. You gave my shirt to that Nazi!"

Although she's almost totally dazed, Patty reminds him that he hadn't even opened the shirt or taken out the packaging pins, and she implies that he has a whole store full of shirts.

The father ignores her remark and continues to pour out the vile and putrid memories of his bitter soul. He speaks of the birth of her younger sister, Sharon, who was so "pale and pretty," and how, then, he had thought that maybe they could be a good family. However, because Patty, even at birth, hated him so much, he can't stand to look at her. He calls her a bad person, and then adds that because she is a Bergen he'll do his duty by her—what's called for. He speaks of the fact that he knows he can't legally cleanse his hands of her, and that the law can't legally call her a traitor, but then he tells her she's done all she can to hurt him. "A person can only stand so much. A man can only try so hard for so long." With complete bewilderment, Patty murmurs, "I never meant to hurt you."

Now, as a rule, I don't generally go around talking to television sets or other inanimate objects. But, I confess, I did that night. The damaging, vile accusations the father laid on his young daughter brought me up out of my chair, and I shouted at our seventeen-inch screen with all my might, "Stop it! Stop doing that to her! Stop telling her those lies!"

The father didn't hear me, of course, so he finished off the scene. I could feel the inner rage boiling in this man as he got nose to nose with his daughter to give her his ultimatum. He pointed out that she would continue to live in his house until she was eighteen, and then, with his mouth curled in utter contempt and hatred, he growled, *"But you . . . you are dead to me, girl!"*

The camera gave a close-up of Patty's face, and you could see the shattering of her whole being as she absorbed the full, forceful blow of her father's words. You also felt that what you had just witnessed was a moment in two people's lives where one human being had just raped another human being's soul. It seemed that nothing would ever be right again.

Patty had been devastated—Humpty Dumpty had fallen

off the wall! The image of the famous nursery-rhyme character materialized in my thoughts, and I realized that in every drawing I've ever seen of him he was always portrayed as an egg. I found myself wondering: Why an egg? Why didn't the now long-gone artists draw Humpty Dumpty as a little elf, a horse, or even a cat? Did they choose an egg to direct our attention to the fragility of life, or our sensitivity to easily shattered feelings, or our vulnerability to a fall? I don't know, but then, and long after I'd watched this scene, the lines of Humpty Dumpty tumbled through my mind:

> Humpty Dumpty sat on a wall
> Humpty Dumpty had a great fall.
> All the king's horses and all the king's men
> Couldn't put Humpty Dumpty together again.

In the concluding scene of the movie, Patty runs from her home and the shattering encounter with her father. She somehow manages to reach the black part of her town. Patty finds Ruth's house and pushes open the screen door.

Ruth is a large black woman. She is the cook and housekeeper who had been fired some time before from the Bergen home because Ruth had defended Patty once too often.

Patty rushes into the kitchen and stumbles into Ruth's open arms. Ruth has heard that the boy is dead and, as she holds Patty in her arms, she strokes her hair and begins to comfort her, for she had known of Patty's feelings for the young German. The gentle love which passes between them is sorely needed by Patty, and the scene is extremely touching.

The girl asks Ruth if she thinks the boy really loved her. Ruth assures her that he did, and confirms it by adding, "I seen it clear as the Christmas star!"

Abruptly then, as she recalls one of her father's remarks,

Patty questions, "How come my mother married my father?"

Before Ruth answered, and in one split second as it were, a small flag raised up in my head and waved in the breezes of my mind. Something whispered, "Listen up—you are going to hear something important." I leaned forward.

Instead of directly answering Patty's question, Ruth holds the girl at arm's length and says, "Now, here . . . when I goes shopping and I sees something marked 'irregular,' I knows that I ain't gonna have to pay so much for it. Girl, you got yourself some irregular folks, and you've been paying top dollar for them all along. So just don't go wastin' up your life wishin' for what ain't gonna be!"

Then Patty, bewilderment and hurt all over her face, counters with what her father said. "He said I was a bad person ever since the day I was born . . . and that I was a dead person, too."

Ruth shakes her head and tells Patty that she isn't bad and she's definitely not dead. She reminds the girl that the soldier knew it, and that she knows it, and she ends with, "An' I'm telling you, Miss Patty Bergen, *we* is the only ones that matter . . . *cause we ain't irregular.* Now, you stand up straight! You is a whole person . . . a creature of God and a thing that matters in this world. Straighten up, girl. You got person-pride from this day on. And I don't *never* wanta see you slopin' your shoulders or your soul again. Not never!"

By the time Patty leaves Ruth, her head is up, her posture straight, and the movie winds up as she walks slowly through the hostile town and heads for home.

Although the screenplay has taken literary license with the book's story, the ending of this remarkable movie was simply and truthfully pointing out that most of us have an irregular person in our lives, and we must not lay the blame for our upbringing on this person. We have to stop reliving

24

the past. But, most of all, we have to stop navel-gazing and spending inordinate amounts of time with daily introspection about our parents or family, *and move on.*

Some mothers, fathers, brothers, sisters, cousins, uncles, aunts, husbands, wives and in-law relatives are just *irregular.* They don't act, react, speak, think or even write the way we would expect them to.

More than one person has come to me after I have spoken on "Irregular People" and has said with obvious relief, "I never knew what to call my mother" . . . "I thought I was the only one in the world to have a father-in-law like mine" . . . "Thank you for telling me I'm not going insane—that I am *regular* and my sister is not" . . . "Today, I have a name for my father, and I finally am able to deal with him, now that I know he is irregular."

It's the same kind of relief when, after weeks of testing or going to several medical specialists, they all agree on what is causing your illness. You're not thrilled that the diagnosis is cancer, lupus, arthritis, or diabetes, but at least now you know *its name,* and you and your doctors can begin to take medical steps to deal with the problem.

A woman who attended my seminar on "Irregular People" wrote:

> Thanks for giving me a more acceptable word to describe those people. Being a therapist, I have to diagnose from among 80 or so different categories of personality and character disorders. It will be much more pleasant for me now when among my friends and acquaintances to mentally classify some as "irregular" rather than paranoid or schizoid, etc.

We attach great significance to names and labels in our world today. How well I know this. When I'm autographing books, I ask for the person's first name and, believe me, it's woe unto me if I sign "To Linda" if the lady spells it "Lynda." She wants the book signed to her—the person who is Lynda—not Linda. I can readily understand this desire to call things and people by their proper names, for we live in a world which works hard at dissolving our original individuality.

Learning from *The Summer of My German Soldier* that these people in our lives are our "irregular" ones brought an enormous sense of relief and a flow of tears which began a releasing process in my own life. The identifying label helped me take my first tottering steps toward dealing with and accepting this person.

The Summer of My German Soldier would never have touched my life the way it did if it had not been that I have had an irregular person for most all of my years. But now, for the first time, because this film had given these people a name, I realized I was not the only one in the world with an irregular person. I sensed the beginnings of a quiet awakening of hope.

CHAPTER TWO

FOR YEARS I'VE HAD TWO MISCONCEPTIONS about irregular people in general. Number one, as I've already stated, I thought no one else had such a person in their lives. And, number two, I imagined that my irregular person was unique and original in his feelings and responses to me. Not so. In fact, your irregular person and mine are probably so much alike they could be twins.

As I began to gather material and do comparison research on these people in our lives, I found that, with few exceptions, they appear to be suffering from many of the same emotional ailments. Irregular people have similar, if not identical, personality traits. Their responses and reactions to us, whether verbal or nonverbal, physical or passive, deliberate or unintentional, fall in the same ruts and follow the same patterns. It's as if they are all hiking along the same well-marked path.

Recently I did a radio program for *Focus on the Family* with my friend, Dr. James Dobson. The subject was "Irregular People." Not long after it aired, the mail began coming in. One very articulate woman wrote Dr. Dobson, "I listened with much interest to your discussion with Joyce Landorf on irregular people. Actually, I cried through the whole program. The Lord has put me in the midst of several irregular people. Sometimes I don't manage too well, and sometimes I don't manage at all.

"Mostly it's so frustrating," she concluded, "because you can't reason with them, can't depend on them, and can't expect any real support from them."

Reading her last statement—"can't reason, can't depend, and can't expect"—was like seeing a group portrait of irregular people at some kind of a family reunion. They all have so many things in common, they appear alike.

I understand people's choice of words when they come to me after I've talked about irregular people, and they speak about *relief*. "I'm so *relieved*," they say, "to know I'm not imagining the things my mother (father, brother, in-laws, husband, wife, etc.) has said or done to me. She (or he) is just like your person." There *is* a genuine relief in finding someone else who knows and understands something about the puzzling, frustrating, even painful conflicts within a family.

The composite picture of irregular people which emerges varies in some of the details involving their actions or comments, and in the experiences of their childhood which have made them irregular in the first place. But, for the most part, irregular people think, respond, and act in very similar patterns.

Here are some of the patterns most irregular people follow. These are the traits which surfaced again and again in my own experience, in conversations, in correspondence, and in research. The first pattern to materialize involved a problem concerning their emotional eyesight.

Irregular People Are Emotionally Blind

They are not physically blind of course, but definitely emotionally blind. What makes this enigma a large square pill to swallow is the fact that, while blind to us, the irregular person can be perfectly capable of seeing other people, their own situations, and their own needs with flawless 20/20 vision.

Actually, it's downright peculiar how selective this emotional blindness can be. For instance, an irregular mother may have a "blind spot" where one of her three children is concerned, or in another case an irregular father may be "blind" to his entire family. Either way, this myopic handicap is terribly hard to understand. If we are to live and cope with this person and their "visual" problems and distorted viewpoints, we must come to the realization that, in order for us to survive, God will have to give us a few healings along the way. And, God be praised, He *does* grant those healings! There is hope for everyone who struggles with the problem of irregular people. If that were not so, I could never have written this book.

Let's move on now and examine this mental and emotional form of blindness. When your irregular person is blind to you, he or she cannot see your talents, skills, or successes in your field of endeavor. He or she cannot see or handle the spiritual, or even the material, gifts the Lord has seen fit to loan you. Sadly, he or she rarely sees you as you really are or recognizes your strengths as being those "special abilities" Paul tells us we all have (1 Cor. 12:4, TLB). Also, many times your irregular person's blindness, especially if they are a grandparent, not only affects you, but extends to your children as well.

Usually, in their blindness, irregular people view someone else's children (or mother, father, niece, nephew, etc.) as smarter, richer, more talented, or—worst of all—*better* people. Comparing other people to you becomes a way of life to your irregular person and adds to your frustration. You realize you can rarely, if ever, please them, so you try harder and run faster, only to find sometimes you aren't even *in* the race, much less a trophy winner!

Here are some real-life examples. They are all true experiences. I've changed or omitted things only to protect the people who so beautifully became vulnerable and shared their irregular persons with me. I'm sure you will begin to

29

understand how the disease of emotional blindness in a relationship is very widespread.

• There are the irregular parents who never attended any of their daughter's swim meets while she was in competition. They were blind to the fact that she broke all the swimming records, in every event, her first year of high school. Later, as a senior, she became the secretary of both her class and the student body, but at no time would either parent acknowledge her accomplishments.

She said of that time, "I tried so hard to make my parents see that I was good." Then, when she had won the title of homecoming queen her senior year, she recalled thinking, *Now they'll be proud of me!* But again, out of blindness, her mother's only cryptic comment was, "I guess it pays to be cheap with the boys." Receiving no affirmation or approval from her parents wreaked havoc in this young girl's heart. She eventually worked through this, but as a teenager she could not understand the blindness of her irregular parents.

• There is an irregular father who was told by many people that his daughter was especially talented in piano and voice, but whenever she performed in musicals or gave recitals, he never attended. Even after she had excelled in music and had several solo albums to her credit, his *only* observation to her was, "You should hear Mrs. Brown play the piano . . . because she can *really* play!"

• There is an irregular mother-in-law who was flown thousands of miles to see her son and daughter-in-law's brand-new dream house. But, after taking the tour, she remained silent. Her son, anxious to hear how she liked it, asked her, but her only comment, "It's too bad you don't have a stainless steel kitchen sink . . .", devastated him.

• There is an irregular grandfather who flew to California from the East to see his daughter's first child. As he held the four-day-old infant in his arms, he announced blindly to his daughter, "You should see your brother's little baby. He's sure smart and cute!" There was never any comment on the baby he was holding in his arms.

• There is an irregular mother-in-law who came to a Christmas dinner at her son and daughter-in-law's house. She brought no food, and contributed no help. She merely surveyed the table laden with all sorts of delicious culinary wonders and blindly whined, "Don'tcha have any plain red jello?"

• There is the irregular mother who took one quick look at her own newborn granddaughter and, out of her own warped vision, said venomously to her son, "She sure doesn't look like you. She must be illegitimate!"

• There is the irregular mother who never seemed to notice that her daughter existed. No bond of any kind was ever established between them. The daughter summed up her childhood by saying, "I just kinda grew up, lived in the same house, did the chores, and made sure I got good grades. I was always referred to as "it" in place of my name. Now, as a Christian adult, the hardest thing is to trust in my worth in God's eyes."

No small wonder she has a problem with accepting herself—having never received any acceptance during her childhood. No wonder she has trouble believing that God truly loves and approves of her. A mother's blindness has made this young woman wary of trusting God's eyesight!

• There are the irregular parents who apathetically did nothing about their son's complicated dental problem, which involved protruding teeth, facial disfigurement, and total malocclusion.

After an emotionally painful childhood, and after constantly being taunted during his teen years, the son married. At age thirty-five, he finally was able to finance his own corrective surgery. The results were both cosmetically pleasing and medically sound, greatly improving his state of physical health. Everyone in the small town where he had lived all his life saw the remarkable outer and inner changes. Everyone, that is, except his mother and father.

His parents remained blind and silent for many months until, out of his bewildering frustration, the son asked them what they thought about his orthodontic work. "You should have spent the money on food for your children," came his mother's only response.

• There is the irregular mother who, though she had two girls, only "saw" one. The invisible daughter confided, "My sister is the only one, in my mother's eyes. I don't even exist when my sister is around. I don't know why it is that I am afraid to talk to my mother about this."

I know why. She's very reluctant to bring this up because, in her lifetime of almost daily rejection, she's become highly allergic to being invisible. The thought of confronting her mother and experiencing yet *another* rejection fills her with a unique kind of dread.

• There is the irregular father who himself is a pastor and has two grown sons in the ministry. His myopia permits him to see only one son—the one who is a missionary. He is blind to the son who is a pastor in town.

At the Christmas-dinner table, this father prayed long and loudly about his beloved son who was "laboring for the Lord on the mission field in that dry foreign land." Next, he prayed on lovingly about the dedication of his sweet daughter-in-law who was out there colaboring by her husband's side.

Then, as the rest of the family listened, the father turned his attention to his *other* son, the pastor of a thriving church, who was seated at the table with his wife. The father prayed, "And then, Lord, there's my son here, and he's just climbin' up fool's hill!"

This father, totally blind to one son while clearly seeing the other son, continues to blunder on through life. He is blithely unaware that he is verbally beating one of his boys to death with the hammer blows of his rejection.

This incredible astigmatism which allows a parent to see one child but not another is a familiar, oft-repeated pattern. A friend of mine wrote, "My mother told me that she thought her firstborn was the most wonderful thing in the whole world, and she worshiped and adored her. She did not want any more children. My sister had filled every desire, but then my dad talked her into having another child because he felt it was not right to raise an only child, so I was born and adored by my father. But I do not ever remember my mother dressing me or combing my hair or bathing me. My daddy did it all for me."

For the most part, this woman was raised as an only child, and of a single parent as well . . . even though, for all appearances, the family looked healthy and normal.

Mother Teresa, who won the Nobel Peace Prize for her work of ministering to the "poorest of the poor" in Calcutta, India, said recently, "In these twenty years of work among the people, I have come more and more to realize that being unwanted is the worst disease any human being can ever experience."

• After my seminar on irregular people, a woman said, "I had always wondered why I didn't care too much for my mother. But, as you talked, I suddenly realized why. For years, every time I've gone to visit her, she has always taken one look at me, sighed, and announced wearily, "Ever since your brothers left home—I've nothing to live for."

• There is the irregular father who regularly phones his writer-daughter and talks only of the book *he* is writing. Other times he points out some woman author and proclaims, "Now, *she's* the best woman writer in the whole Christian field," or he reads several paragraphs to her from someone's newly published book and practically shouts, *"That's real writing!"* Yet, he remains blind to his daughter's own widely circulated books, and, *if* he has read any of them, he steadfastly refuses (or is unable) to comment on them one way or another.

Besides all of the hundreds of hurts the irregular person's blindness inflicts, it becomes even more complicated because of this next pattern.

Irregular People Are Emotionally Deaf

I'm not sure that all irregular people start out with an emotional hearing impairment, or even if they suspect they have such a hearing loss, but with time, their hearing ability seems to decline at a very rapid pace. And a hearing loss to some degree of intensity is an all-too-common pattern. It is as though here and there in the irregular person's mind, big chunks of denial block or plug their heart's ability to hear.

Once in a while you'll have a "fairly normal" conversation with your irregular person, in which he or she seems to see and hear quite well. When that happens, you are so pleased that you eagerly plunge ahead and boldly share something which is of vital importance, only to find you are not talking to a living, breathing human being, but to a stone mask. A sudden and profound deafness has overtaken them, and instant denial sets up like cement in their ears to block out everything you've just said.

In Bette Green's book, *Summer of My German Soldier*, she tells of a moment when Patty's father is about to beat her—verbally and physically—for breaking a rule. She begs him to let her explain what happened and why. But the father just keeps coming at her. She writes of the moment, "It [her pleading] was just noise to him. A mask cannot really hear."

Again, here are some illustrations, taken from real life, about the extraordinary toll emotional deafness extracts from a relationship.

• A woman in her early thirties discovered a lump in her breast. When all the medical tests were completed, the results showed that she had a malignancy. A radical mastectomy was scheduled for the next week.

She knew she had never been able to talk with her mother. ("She *never* listens to me!") But, because of the seriousness of the surgery, she felt that for once her mother would *have* to listen. She called and made a luncheon date.

Cautiously, as she drove her mother home from lunch, the daughter began. "I've a lump . . . all the tests show . . . next Tuesday, a mastectomy. . . ."

After a few moments of electric silence and no reaction whatsoever from her mother, the woman bluntly asked if she had heard what was said. The mother nodded her head affirmatively and, as if her daughter had merely read off the charges on her phone bill, calmly dismissed the whole subject. Then, with animation, she said, "You know, your sister has the best chicken enchilada recipe. I'll have to give it to you."

The daughter pulled the car over and, with mounting frustration, yelled, "*Mother*, I just told you I have cancer. I may die, and I'm scared to death of this surgery . . ."

Her mother was fairly indignant that her daughter had shouted at her. She reminded her not to use "that" tone of voice—"after all, the Bible says to honor thy father and mother."

Utterly furious, the daughter screamed, *"Why don't you hear me?"* With an unearthly detachment from reality, the mother calmly responded, "You need to know, also, that if you leave the enchiladas in the oven too long, they dry out and get hard."

This mother was suffering from an irreversible case of emotional deafness—irreversible, that is, but for God.

• Another young woman wrote, "I heard you so clearly tonight. Especially when you told the enchilada story. I had a similar experience. My home and marriage were breaking up, my girls were in trouble, and I was hurting like I'd never hurt before in all my life. About the time when things were at their worst, I tried to share with my mother-in-law. I told her that her son and I were separating after twenty-three years of marriage. She looked right past me and, as if I'd said nothing at all, she serenely reflected, "Oh, isn't it a lovely sunset?"

Denial is both blind and deaf, and we are acutely aware of it at the most inopportune moments of our lives.

• An attractive young wife told me how utterly crushed and shattered she had been when she accidentally discovered that her husband was having an affair. Immediately, she rushed over to her mother's home and bared her heart. The mother, in the extreme deafness of denial, only chided, "Your hair looks terrible. You really need to fix it up a bit." That remark closed the door forever on the subject.

Whenever we say what's really on our hearts, we open up our very souls, and the vulnerability of it all is extreme. To share with the blind and deaf irregular person in our life, to be so terribly vulnerable, and then to be unseen and unheard is devastating. It's akin to being shot down over a war zone, bailing out and landing in a mine field; having both legs blown off, and then not dying, but being taken to a P.O.W. camp for the duration of the war.

"Wait a minute, Joyce," I can hear you say. "Isn't that example laying it on too thick?"

I think not. I've opened up my heart, become vulnerable time and time again, only to feel the terrible pains of rejection! I keep telling myself, "They *will* see me, they *will* hear me, they have just *got* to. It's abnormal not to see and hear . . ." But it doesn't happen. The problem goes on and on.

Not only are irregular people blind and deaf, but they have other serious communication problems.

Irregular People Have Badly Damaged Vocal Chords

I'm never quite sure how those vocal chords have been damaged, or by whom. I only know that to communicate is an impossibility. They are severely handicapped. While they *can* verbally speak, irregular people mix up their vocabulary and generally manage to say all the wrong words at the wrong times.

The one pattern which seems to be the easiest to discern is the one involving apologies. Irregular people simply cannot bring themselves, for whatever reason, to the point of accepting the responsibility for something which has gone wrong. Hence, they cannot ask *anyone's* forgiveness. Apologizing is not within the realm of possibility for them.

An irregular person perceives himself or herself as never having failed, as never being capable of making a mistake, and certainly as never saying anything that could be construed as inaccurate or stupid. Someone *else* is always at fault, someone else is always blamed, and someone else always needs to apologize.

Some psychologists call this trait in the irregular person

the "no-faulter" concept. They point out that no-faulters are basically insecure people. These people are highly resistant to change, and will not accept responsibility for any action.

I think my own irregular person is constantly struggling and striving for approval and for a lofty degree of credibility. For him, to leave the keys locked up in his car, to be late, to get lost when going somewhere, or to have no instantaneous answer to give is deeply jarring—and it almost demands that he immediately blame someone else.

A dear friend of mine finally called her irregular mother the other day. In assertive but gracious tones, she listed all the annoying, inconsiderate, and unloving things her mother had done in recent months.

My friend sent me a copy of her mother's letter after that conversation. It was priceless.

The letter was a perfect example of a no-faulter's position, for it started with placing the blame on the daughter in the second sentence. Then, almost every paragraph included questions like, "There isn't much else I can say, is there?" and another classic, "I can't help that, can I?"

Then the letter ended with the suggestion that it was really up to the *daughter* to accept this behavior and the incidents, unacceptable as they are, because the mother felt *she'd* been acting perfectly normally. Then she turned super-spiritual, and one of her last lines read, "Negative feelings can be quieted by reading Ephesians 4:31–32."

There you have the Christian no-faulter's answer to conflict within relationships. No blame assumed, just preachments about how the *other* person should change.

This "no-faulter" behavior is so ingrained in irregular people that they act as if the whole world is out to get them. Try riding in a car when your irregular person is driving, and count how many times you hear, "Did you see that guy? He nearly sideswiped my car! . . . I had the right-of-way. . . . What's that fool doing?"

Irregular people are also easily offended. To my horror, so am I—at times, I believe, more so than other people. I think it's unbecoming of me to be easily offended, and I'm truly trying to listen to the Holy Spirit so that my life will live out the fruits of the Spirit. However, the difference here is that when the irregular person is in the wrong, he or she refuses to admit it, or to take any responsibility for what is happening. They rarely say, "I blew it!" or, "Wow, I misjudged that man," or "I'm sorry, this was my fault and I accept the blame."

Who was it that said, "Of all the most difficult words in the English language, the hardest are 'I was wrong and you were right!'"? They were certainly accurate.

Bishop William Connor Magee once wrote, "The man who makes no mistakes does not usually make anything." I'd have to amend that a bit to read, "The man or woman who makes no mistakes makes a lot of trouble for all the rest of us."

Right here I'm going to stop and ask you to consider something. It may be important, so don't skip this part.

Perhaps, when you began this book, you searched your mind to see if you had an irregular person in your life. You didn't *think* you did, but now that you're reading this chapter and I'm describing the patterns usually found in irregular people you are pretty *sure* you have escaped the irregular person. You are not related to anyone who fits these descriptions. Except that swirling around in the back of your head you have the strange feeling you do know *someone* who well *may* be irregular . . . and with a slight sinking of heart, you are wondering if I have been describing *you* and *your* patterns of behavior towards someone else in your family.

A woman thanked me for my "Irregular People" seminar because, in the middle of it, she realized with clarity and God-given insight that she was rapidly *becoming* an irregular person to her ten-year-old daughter. Another woman said she was horrified to realize she had been blaming her husband for all the problems in their marriage, when it was *she* who followed the patterns of the irregular person to the letter.

In yet another seminar, a mother and daughter sat listening. The daughter told me later that during my talk she wondered how she could tell her mother (sitting right next to her) that she (the mother) was the irregular person in her own life. At that exact moment, the mother leaned over and whispered, *"My* mother was my irregular person, and I just realized that I may be your irregular person. Could this be?" The daughter nodded yes, and the mother continued, "Then let's not let this happen . . ." The daughter shared later that a few minutes after the meeting she and her mother had begun talking. It had been the first honest verbal communication of their lives, and a healing had begun.

So, if you have started suspecting that you might be following the patterns of the irregular person, stop here and now. Thank the Lord for the Holy Spirit's conviction, and begin to realize that you're halfway home to healing and changing one of life's most crippling relationships. You have just laid the problem out on the table, and now you can take steps to deal with it. The *truly* irregular person rarely is able to *ever* see himself, or herself, as irregular to anybody—so you've taken a giant step forward in healing a relationship with someone you love.

Now, back to damaged vocal chords, and the irregular person's difficulty with communicating an apology. You see, in order to apologize, we first have to admit that *we* made a mistake or did something wrong, and most of us find that enormously humbling. Irregular people cannot afford any admission of a mistake or wrongdoing, nor can they handle the trauma of having made an error. It's almost as if they were saying, "If I admit my mistake, people

40

won't like me." So humbling themselves and apologizing is rarely within their framework of responses.

• A woman whose husband is the irregular person to her and her children wrote to Dr. James Dobson following a radio broadcast on the irregular person:

> My husband has great difficulty in being a father and a husband. It is only in the last few years that he has even acknowledged to me that he "thinks" he has a problem. Last week he apologized to our twenty-year-old daughter, and said that the argument they had was his fault! That was a big miracle, and I thank God for it.

In that same letter, I quickly determined this woman's sense of humor was alive and well when she mused,

> Sometimes I think irregular people should only marry each other, and they should never have any children.

I stopped smiling, however, and sobered immediately, when she added that a few years ago her teenage son had committed suicide because of the difficult relationship with his father. This perceptive woman said of her husband, "I know he would like to be different, but his own scars are so deep."

I can readily understand how the father's apology to their daughter not too long ago was described by this mother as "a big miracle." Her letter to Dr. Dobson ends with,

> I'm sure the Lord knows what He is doing, but I am looking forward to Joyce Landorf's book. There must be something more I can learn that will be helpful in dealing with these irregular people in my life. One thing sure, these people keep me on my knees, and maybe the Lord knows I need to stay there!"

Another problem with damaged vocal chords and blocked communication lines is the fact that your irregular person has a difficult time praising you or finding something good to say about you. Irregular people's own feelings of self-worth are so low they have a need to keep everyone else's confidence at that same low level.

• A woman writes of her irregular mother-in-law and says,

> She has never complimented me when I play the piano, yet it has been my profession for sixteen years. She also never compliments my husband (her son) whenever he does anything special.
> She does say, "I love you," but the way in which she says it throws guilt all over us. She tells us we never visit her enough or stay long enough or, when she lives with us two weeks each winter, we don't take her enough places. She also wants to know why we don't cancel our "ridiculous schedule" to stay home with her. Her "I love yous" always say, "But you don't love me that much back."

This woman's letter ends with these poignant words: "We want to love, honor, respect, and uphold my dear Christian mother-in-law, but the relationship is buried in negatives, and I don't think she even realizes it."

The irregular person's inability-to-praise pattern is followed closely by a great talent for criticizing. I wish this were not so. But the lower one's own self-esteem sinks, the lower one's own self-respect drops, the higher the need seems to be to verbally take others apart.

• A pastor's wife wrote of her irregular person's characteristics and patterns. This is quite a long letter, but I want to share it with you. Candidly she explained,

> My irregular person is my mother. She has been my irregular person since my early childhood. My father died when I

was four, in an automobile accident, and that, along with a very unhappy childhood herself, has caused her to be a very bitter, negative person. Mother never, to my knowledge, hugged or kissed me as a child, nor has she ever said, "I love you." I can remember the words "I HATE you," when she would get particularly angry at me for some reason. Then she would apologize and say, "I really didn't mean that." But still, I had great pity for her—she never let us forget that she was alone in this world and that we had to help her. I never got a good-night kiss, or whispered words of praise when I excelled in something.

And, oh, how hard I tried to do my very best to please her. I cooked and cleaned, and helped care for my brothers, and tried to never cause her any worry or care. All through my teen years, thanks be to God for a strong church and some wonderful Christian families who showed me what Christian living was all about, I was able to remain a firm witness for Christ. Yet she was always accusing me of necking, or "going all the way with a boy," when the truth of the matter was we were only friends. But with her hot temper and stubbornness, you could never convince her she was wrong. All through my teenage years, I was torn between loving her and hating her. Then came the time for me to go away to college. I was surprised that she let me go. But I had a scholarship and, in spite of her strange ways of showing it, I knew she loved me and wanted the best for me.

In college, this young woman met the man she wanted to marry, and four years later she did marry him. However, even that happy occasion was not without trauma. Her letter continued:

On the day we told my mother of our engagement, she pouted and would not speak to us for three days. She finally realized that she was not going to be able to keep me at home to take care of her, so she put all of her energies into making a beautiful wedding for me. But the days before our wedding she resented any time I spent with my fiancé, and the night before she cried and threw a terrible fit because I wanted my husband-to-be with us for supper and she wanted me to herself. On the day of the wedding, never once did she hug me and do all the things mothers of the brides are supposed to do, or tell me all the delicious intimacies that mothers and daughters do. As we left, and the rice was being thrown, she was standing off in a corner sobbing.

And the letter concluded with a here-and-now comment on her mother's attitudes and actions:

My mother says my house is always filthy, I'm partial to one of my children, I never dress right, and I do not act in a manner befitting a preacher's wife. I have never received a compliment on a ladies' lecture or seminar I've delivered, or for an honor that has been bestowed upon me in my teaching profession. Also, my children have never received a compliment from her.

• Another woman confided, "I've finally worked through my bitterness with my irregular grandmother, even though she always said I was 'rotten to the core'."

• My friend Reuben Welch, in his sensitive and deeply moving book, *We Really Do Need Each Other*, writes,

You would not believe some of the letters
  that students show me from their parents.
And parents wouldn't believe
  that students show them to me, either.
I read letters that say in all kinds of ways—
    "I don't trust you
    you aren't good
    when will you ever change
you are always late, why don't you write
  you aren't responsible
  you are a disappointment
after all we've done for you,
  you'll have to get married—
    you'll get pregnant."

I have seen the long arm of parental control and judgment
   reach across the miles from home to dormitory
and almost destroy the precious
     growing, seeking life
     of a young college student.

• One young woman related for me how difficult it was to please her irregular father. She feared his impatience with her more than anything else. Whenever he worked around the house fixing something, and needed some tool, he would call and tell her to go out to the garage to get it for him. She'd go out and rummage frantically around the garage searching for the tool, knowing that if she returned empty-handed her dad would take in a large volume of air, breathe out a very disgusted sigh, storm out of the house to the garage, and bring the tool back with him. Then, as predictable as the sunrise, he'd shout, *"If it was a snake, it would have bitten you!"*

Perhaps that's not such a bad thing to have yelled at you (if you compare it with other abusive sentiments), but couple that with a *total lack* of any praise, repeat the phrase enough times, and . . . the damage will be permanent.

• In a beautiful, highly detailed letter, a twenty-three-year-old woman spoke of her years of growing up. She wrote:

> I grew up in a large family and my father is a pastor and teaches at a Bible school. My mother died suddenly, without any warning, when I was nine. My father is irregular. He'd do just about anything for anyone in the church or at school. But he's never had time or shown concern for his children. Although he does a lot of marriage counseling, he is an emotional infant, at least to his family. I have a great deal of respect for his knowledge of the Word, his dedication to good works, but I pity him for what he has missed with his family.

He cannot express his feelings to us in even a small way. He has seven children, all of whom he has every reason to be proud of—talented, love-the-Lord, friendly, lovable kids. Yet he cannot tell any of us that he approves, that he's proud or pleased with us. Incidentally, he doesn't let us know if he's displeased either.

Each of my four brothers and two sisters has their tale. One brother is a professional singer (tenor) with a large midwest symphony, and has the best voice. He's given many recitals and concerts, and my father will not go to them. My Dad will stay away from a church conference he'd normally attend when my brother is the guest singer!! Another brother is an M.D. with a heart of compassion for people. He graduated cum laude from Yale, and has longed for a positive word from Dad. Not one. Same down the line, with each son or daughter. My oldest sister has the most adorable kids, but they hardly know their granddad.

Later in her letter, she accurately described the damaged-vocal-chord syndrome when she told me how one time a friend had said to her father and stepmother, "Your daughter did the most bang-up job of programing music at camp. *You should see* the rapport she has with those girls. They just hung on her when it was time to go!"

They gave her a brief smile and said, "Oh, really?" And then when we got home, my stepmother said, "My, isn't it interesting how people think you're so wonderful? Well, you're not so wonderful at home, are you?"

Besides not being able to apologize or give praise, another communication problem irregular people have is the tendency to be threatened by even the simplest question. It's almost as if your asking a question is an indictment of their authority or, at the very least, a defiant contradiction.

Bette Green, in *Summer of My German Soldier*, wrote,

"In my father's vocabulary, to ask why is to contradict him."

I have only just recently learned to rephrase my questions so that I can ask something of my irregular person without *appearing* to ask. It's no easy trick, and I always approach the problem the way porcupines make love—very carefully. Years ago, if I asked, "Are you coming for Christmas dinner?" my irregular person would cough, clear his throat, and then mumble a great deal.

What was really just a simple question could not be simply answered. Irregular people are deeply threatened by a bold-faced proposal. Perhaps it's because deep down they know they have *answered* incorrectly, or whatever, in the past—and now they've got to come up with a *right* answer so as not to appear diminished in any capacity.

• When the irregular parents of a college girl were called and asked, "Are you coming to see your daughter when she gets crowned homecoming queen?" the answer was, "Well, ah, no. We have other plans. My wife has to have her hair done."

• When asked why she couldn't come to her grandson's baby shower, an irregular mother-in-law explained that she had to stay home and let the washing-machine repairman in (even though her husband would be home at the time).

Did you ever get a mental block when you were taking a quiz or a final exam? I have. And this seems to be exactly what happens to irregular people. They seem to freeze. Remember, I said that they can't take the responsibility of being wrong, nor can they accept the blame. Well, this is one reason a direct question sends an irregular person into a tailspin. Then, in order to avoid answering, even the Christian irregular person often lies. After several years of

47

watching it happen, I know almost in advance when I'm going to hear a distortion of the truth. Irregular people cannot be found wanting—in any area—so they compensate with a made-up story. Being wrong is simply terrifying to no-faulter people, so they build up rigid walls of defense to rule out blame.

Nowadays, I don't ask, "Are you coming for Christmas dinner?" I merely lay it open for discussion with something like, "We are planning to have Christmas dinner at 4:00 P.M. on December 25. We'd love to have you come, but you don't have to give me an answer just now." Sometimes it even works.

Perhaps the most hurtful breach in the communication department is that irregular people simply cannot verbally express love and approval.

The same twenty-three-year-old girl I wrote of earlier said, near the end of her letter, that she knew she was loved by teachers, friends, and especially by a couple in her church who had been virtually a family to her. Yet, she wrote, "My heart cries out for the approval of my father. I told my adopted dad, "I know you love me, and I love you too, but I need to hear my natural dad say he loves me."

My heart breaks for all of us who would dearly love to have acceptance and approval from irregular parents, brothers, sisters-in-law, and so on, but at the same time I feel sad for the irregular people themselves. How awful to be so crippled in our spirits that we cannot express love or give acceptance freely.

• A woman married over thirty years recalled that when she was very little she had wanted up on her mother's lap, but she had been told, "No, I can't hold you. You hurt my knees."

That mother may have had a real physical problem with damaged knees, but all her little girl heard was, "*You* hurt my knees." Rejection, even at an early age, that is expressed one way or another on a day-to-day basis, doesn't need to be spelled out. It just drapes itself around us like a mantle of doom, and is *never* forgotten.

• A woman told me that she went to the hospital for some tests and was told that her father-in-law had just been brought in and was very ill. She said, "I didn't know that he was sick, so I rushed down the hall to see him. However, my irregular mother-in-law reminded me that *only family* was permitted to see him. They wouldn't let me in."

• A highly sensitive child grew up with the easy ability for tears. She was able to cry readily until her irregular father's remark, "She flushes easily," convinced her she was being compared to a toilet, and the sting of rejection scarred and burnt her heart to a cinder. For many years she would allow no tears whatsoever to flow.

Once when I said publicly that my irregular person has rarely, if ever, said "I love you" directly to me, a woman wrote what I call a *solution letter*. She said that with my darling, outgoing personality (ta-da!) I should just get my irregular person alone and, looking straight at him, tell him that I loved him, and "then he will just *melt* and say right back, 'Joyce, I love you!' "

It sounded simple enough, and at that time in my relationship I'd worked through *many* feelings and was to the point where I could *honestly*, with no reservations, say I loved him. So I did what the lady said. It was Christmas, and late in the day I was alone with him in the living room. I put my arms around his neck, looked him right in the eyes, wished him a merry Christmas and a blessed New Year, and ended with, "I want you to know—I love you!" He smiled faintly and, nodding his head, he said, "Two-way street."

It was as close as his emotional health would let him come to verbalizing his love. I have *no doubt* that he does

49

indeed love me, but his spirit is so crippled and atrophied with time and experiences that the very best he could say was "Two-way street," in place of the words "I love you." I will never forget the sadness of that moment, or the understanding which broke through to my soul.

I'm sure that much of the time irregular people have no idea of the continual hurts inflicted by the darts they hurl. Sometimes they do know, but can't (or won't) stop the verbal or nonverbal abuse.

One friend said, "Irregular people don't merely 'bug' us—they wound, stab, pull out chunks of our heart, and the poison darts hit deeper as the relationship continues. Verbal and nonverbal abuse leaves invisible scars *and* a feeling of emptiness that is as big as the Grand Canyon."

So it is with the patterns of an irregular person. The disease is rampant, the hurts monumental, but there is hope. Read on . . .

CHAPTER THREE

HAVE YOU EVER WONDERED how long these shattering, turbulent, and irregular relationships have been going on? I sure have. So one day not too long ago I decided to scan the Bible and see if I could spot any of the irregular patterns I have just described.

I never made it past Genesis. There were enough examples in that one book alone to substantiate the fact that the problem of irregular people has been going on since the beginning of time.

• Listen to Adam, after he has eaten of the forbidden fruit, as he explains to God just whose fault this all is. . . . "The woman whom *thou* gavest to be with me, *she* gave me fruit of the tree, and I ate" (Gen. 3:12, RSV, italics added). Then, when the Lord turns to Eve and asks her how she could have done such a thing, she counters with, "The serpent tricked me" (Gen. 3:13, TLB).

Both Adam and Eve display the irregular trait and pattern of people who cannot and will not accept responsibility for their actions. Adam blames God for giving him Eve in the first place, and then accuses her of making him eat the fruit. Eve simply blames the snake. Also, do you notice that *nobody* apologizes?

I've often wondered how God's plan would have been altered, right then and there, in the real garden-spot of the world, if these two newly born sinners would have said, "I, Adam, first child of God, blew it! Forgive me." Or, if Eve had confessed, "I listened to the serpent and I disobeyed and broke your rules, Lord, . . . I'm sorry!"

Instead, the irregular concept of never-if-ever apologizing was put into practice. Both Adam and Eve were blind to their responsibilities to be obedient to God and to seek His forgiveness. Actually, they were also deaf as to really *hearing* what God was saying. Had they truly listened, the serpent would have never been able to transpose God's words to sound like truth. Eve would have countered to Satan, "But that's *not* what God said!" Only she had been deaf to God's instructions. So, back in the very beginning, Adam and Eve modeled those irregular traits that are still with us today.

• Next we have Cain. A man so irregular in his relationship with his younger brother, Abel, that eventually his anger, hatred and spirit of revenge channeled itself into murder. Read on . . .

• In Abraham's life it isn't too hard to identify his irregular person as his nephew, Lot. Since the land did not furnish enough pasture for the flocks of both Abraham and Lot, a very great dispute arose. Abraham, to put an end to the strife, proposed that Lot choose whatever land he wanted. The choice was simple. Lot's irregular, greedy, and selfish nature caused him to choose the very best of the land, leaving his Uncle Abraham with the poorest.

• Lot's wife was quite likely his irregular person. She probably loved Lot, but was so enamored of their lifestyle—the comforts and the social whirl of the twin cities of Sodom and Gomorrah—that it is possible she and Lot had a big argument about leaving. She ignored, or was deaf to, her husband's warning, and turned around for one last look. This time her defiance of Lot and of God's instructions caused her death.

• Beginning in the sixteenth chapter of Genesis, we find the story of Sarah, Abraham's wife, her Egyptian handmaiden, Hagar, and the sons of these two women, Isaac and Ishmael. This tale of tangled, irregular relationships runs on like a soap opera! My editor, Floyd Thatcher, after reading my complicated and lengthy description of this story, wrote me:

> If I'm reading the sequence properly, Hagar, after she got pregnant, was irregular toward Sarah. Then Sarah responded irregularly by being so hard on Hagar that she ran away. . . . Hagar returned after meeting with the angel and continued living with Abraham and Sarah. (It isn't hard to believe that Sarah nursed deep irregular feelings throughout the successive years.) Next, Isaac is born and, sometime after he was weaned (two years), Ishmael became an irregular person to his half-brother by making fun of him. And it was Ishmael's actions, plus Sarah's pent-up feelings, that caused the final desperate action of separation.

I think Floyd got it right!

• The twin sons of Isaac, Jacob and Esau, were plagued with an irregular relationship even before they were born: "The children struggled together within her" (Gen. 25:22, RSV). After they were grown, Jacob's irregular personality and well-known deception caused his brother Esau to lose his highly prized birthright.

• When Jacob married Rachel, it was almost as if God was evening the score, because Jacob had to do serious reckoning with Laban, his irregular father-in-law. Laban turned out to be a man who tricked, deceived, and out-maneuvered Jacob almost as well as Jacob had managed with his own brother Esau.

Barrenness played an essential role in Rachel's life, as it had done in Sarah's. Rachel had to deal with her feelings as her fertile sister, Leah, gave birth to one baby after another. Was theirs an irregular relationship? You betcha!

• Jacob was irregular to the ten sons his wife Leah gave him in that he was blind to all of them. He could only "see" Joseph, Rachel's son. While he knew he had ten other sons (and, later, Benjamin), it was as though only Joseph really mattered or was of any value.

• Then, as Genesis closes, there is the most classic of all illustrations about the irregular person syndrome: Joseph.

Fantastic Joseph. He's the one we all like to remember as being the darling boy depicted as wearing the (usually) striped coat, and then later becoming the prime minister of Egypt. But we sort of glide over the disturbing facts which are: he was rejected, loved, despised and honored, all at the same time, for the first seventeen years of his life.

Jacob loved and adored Joseph so much that he singled him out—heaping honors and a glorious (not merely striped) nobleman's long tunic on him.

The ten half-brothers stood by, smoldering in anger, and when unable to say anything to their father because of his position of authority, they unleashed their hatred on Joseph the first time they got him away from Jacob's tents. They became ten irregular people to Joseph and their open rejection must have utterly devastated him.

Think of that! Joseph was rejected by ten—count 'em, *ten*—vengeful half-brothers, and they would have surely killed him had not the plan of God been otherwise.

Long before I actually sat down and began writing the biblical novel, *Joseph,* I did a year of reading (fifty-three books in all), traveled to Egypt, and tried my best to do my homework on this incredible story. Over and over I was struck by three things:

1. The behavior patterns of the ten half-brothers, with their intense hatred and predictable rejection of Joseph, was as real and prevalent in their family so many thousands of years ago, as it is now. Same song, just a different verse.

2. Joseph's attitude—one of complete, unswerving obedience to his father, Jacob, and to his heavenly Father, God—was as rare and fresh in a person then as it is today.

3. And, lastly, there was the all-consuming knowledge that the same sovereign God who planned out Joseph's days then is still the same one who plans yours and mine this very moment.

• Before Genesis closes out, we read of Judah (fourth son of Jacob and Leah), who grows up and becomes an irregular father-in-law to his son's wife, Tamar. Read the story for yourself in chapter 38. It's pretty sticky, and Tamar's method of confrontation with Judah defies description.

• Finally, as we come to the forty-ninth chapter of Genesis, we find some very perceptive words spoken by Jacob as he is about to die. He gives each one of his sons his blessings (or his curses), and when he comes to Joseph, he gives everyone to understand that he *knows* how grievous the irregular brothers made life for Joseph. So part of his blessing to Joseph speaks powerfully of the rejection shown Joseph by those irregular brothers. "Joseph is a fruitful bough, a fruitful bough by a spring, whose branches run over the wall," Jacob says on his deathbed. "The archers sorely harassed him and shot at him; they have hated him; but his bow remains steady; his arms and his hands are reinforced by the aid of the Mighty God of Jacob, from the Shepherd, the Rock of Israel. . . ." (Gen. 49:22–26).

If these few examples (and, believe me, there are many, many more) tell us anything at all, it is that if irregular people have been around from the time of Adam and Eve, they will be around until the Lord puts his foot down and says, "Enough is enough!"

I have been comforted by the knowledge gleaned from Genesis that if God allowed His people, His *chosen* people, to live and learn through difficult family relationships, then surely *we* can learn.

I have also given some thought as to who Jesus' irregular person might have been. Did that person come from among His twelve disciples, with whom He had a "brother" relationship? This was purely conjecture on my part, but I rather fantasized that it was Peter—*great* Peter—who was, however, blind and deaf to life's subtleties.

He was always saying the wrong thing, doing the wrong thing at exactly the wrong time. I figured because Jesus kept inquiring, "Who am I?" and "Lovest thou me?" that Peter's words and actions must have left a lot to be desired; he was probably a very standard irregular person.

However, today I'm not so sure it was Peter.

As she finished typing the final draft of this chapter, my secretary, Sheila, penned this note to me:

Joyce—
As I type this book, everyone is beginning to look a little irregular to me. . . .

When I typed your third chapter, I was studying chapters 12 and 13 of John. My first thought was—*Judas*—the perfect irregular!

All through Jesus' ministry He loved that man. Judas heard the sermons, observed the miracles, and lived with Jesus, but never *really* heard or saw a thing, and doubtless he returned little warmth or love.

When Judas gave Mary a bad time about the cost of the perfume, it occurred to me that Jesus must have had to contend with remarks like that from Judas all through His ministry.

In our Bible study we were asked to cite all the places in chapter 13 where Jesus showed love to Judas and gave him opportunity to repent. Amazing! To think—Jesus washed those dirty feet, shared meals with him, gave him the "honored sop," withheld his identity as the betrayer from the others, etc., etc., all the while knowing Judas was irregular.

These chapters took on a new meaning for me as I began to see Judas more clearly. I saw how Satan took advantage of his irregular tendencies and how Jesus responded to an irregular person. . . .

Most of this book is an attempt to help us all, and it's not really important to ascertain who Jesus' irregular person was—only, as Sheila wrote, to see "how Jesus responded to an irregular person."

I believe we can trust our God. He will bring us through the difficult situations that arise with our families.

But I have not *always* seen it in this manner. I have not *always* believed God would bring us through, and I have not *always* thought that there was any hope at all. Sometimes the darts that were shot at me were too numerous to dig out—too poisonous to stop the infection, too painful to ever believe I'd survive.

In my letter to you at the beginning of this book, I related that about eight years ago my awareness of a personal irregular relationship in my life came to a head during a family dispute.

I remember my feelings on that fateful day . . . I thought, TODAY WE HAVE PRIED OPEN THE WORST CAN OF WORMS POSSIBLE, AND FROM NOW ON THERE WILL BE NO WAY TO SHOVE ALL THOSE SQUIRMING WORMS BACK INTO THE CAN. WE'LL NEVER BE ABLE TO RESEAL THE LID, PICK UP OUR LIVES, AND GO ON AS IF THE

WORMS IN THAT CAN DO NOT EXIST. BUT MOST OF ALL, HOW DO I COPE WITH ALL THESE WORMS?

There was a day, so many years before, when my marriage was in shambles and I was prepared to slice my wrists open. No day had ever equalled its horror—but this one managed to come quite close.

I recall that the April afternoon eight years ago, weatherwise, and even healthwise, was absolutely glorious.

Our son, Rick, had definitely decided that he and lovely Teresa Pursell would get married. They chose August 18, and we began making plans.

No flag was raised that day to foretell the approaching storm, no misgivings or second thoughts, just a surging of joy. Our son was young, but he had made a mature decision, and we had no reservations about the upcoming marriage.

The day the date was set, my irregular person and his wife unexpectedly dropped in on me for a visit. I was bubbling over with the news that Rick was getting married to Teresa. Our daughter, Laurie, was there and we were excitedly spelling out all the plans for the wonderful wedding.

Suddenly I became very aware that our nearly hysterical expressions of joy were not being shared—at least there was a noticeable cooling of enthusiasm on the part of my irregular person and his wife.

Now a real flag waved in my mind. Not at all sure of how to begin, I asked timidly, "Aren't you pleased about Rick and Teresa?"

The answer came. "Yes, but . . ."

"What do you mean, 'Yes, but'?" The red flag in my mind was joined by several other red flags.

"Well, it's just that August 18 is a bad date. We have to be at a family picnic."

"But it's only April," I cried. "Surely you can arrange to

change or postpone the picnic for an August wedding."

No, as a matter of fact, they couldn't. The picnic, it seemed, was far more important.

Instantly my mind went back to all the important times in my life when I needed (or at least would have loved to have seen) my irregular person. The plays I was in, the musicals, the recitals, and my graduations. But he always had someone else to see or somewhere else to be. When I was younger, I had tried telling myself that he loved me and that it was just the line of work he was in that made me and others in my family come in second. Later, I had rationalized that his priorities were just different from other men.

But on this fine April day, in the midst of my joy, I could not see any love in him, nor could I, in view of past history, rationalize away what he had said.

Everything exploded within me. Screaming into my brain and running rampant in my bloodstream were the words, YOU'RE NOT COMING TO RICK'S WEDDING BECAUSE OF A PICNIC? A *PICNIC?* So I yelled them at him and his wife.

This was one afternoon when I *definitely* know I did *not* possess even one of the fruits of the Spirit. I lost love, joy, peace, longsuffering, gentleness, and meekness, all in one impressive moment, and certainly I abandoned all self-control!

For the better part of two hours I verbalized one "Why?" after another. Didn't he know that Rick was no high-school dropout, no drug addict, no juvenile delinquent, but a marvelous young man who loved God, was on the dean's list for his high grades, and was marrying a terrific Christian girl he'd met at the Youth-for-Christ staff retreat?

My questions and whys were met, initially, with knowing smiles and patronizing looks. At one point, my irregular person turned to Laurie and said with a twisted sense of humor, "Don't you wish your mother was as cool and calm as I am?" (Laurie never answered, because you can't talk when you're sobbing.)

After an hour or so, I realized that he was not listening— or, if he was, he was not *hearing* me. HOW COULD I GET HIM TO HEAR ME? I questioned. Then I knew. I could get his attention if I used a word I don't use in my ordinary daily vocabulary. It is not profanity, but it is coarse. (Paul says not to use profanity or even coarse language, so it's not my habit or custom to use it, except that at that moment I was desperately hoping my irregular person would hear me.) So I looked him straight in the eyes and said clearly, *"Dammit, listen to me!"*

If I had turned into a real, live, 250-pound tiger about to spring on him, I could not have evoked more horror. He walked over to me and did, without a doubt, the most inexplicable thing. He took his thumb and wiped the lipstick off my bottom lip and said, "Anyone who wears this stuff doesn't know Jesus. You'd better get right with God!"

His words were so out of context and so irrelevant to our argument that they caught me off-balance and, for one moment, I laughed.

"I thought we settled the 'sin' of lipstick thirty years ago," I said. He didn't think I was funny and went on, over and over again, telling me how sinful I was.

Strange how one word opened a portion of his hearing, but kept the rest of him deaf to the real issue.

Finally I walked to the front door, opened it, and said, with truly a broken heart, "I'm sorry, but I am talking in Chinese and you are answering me in Swahili. We can't talk or hear each other. Please go."

"You're *throwing* me out of your house!" *He* was shouting now.

"No. We simply cannot communicate. And, furthermore—we never have."

In my whole life, I'd never known what the problem was

between us, or even if there *was* a problem—but in one afternoon, the proverbial can of worms was opened and the agony of it all began to penetrate my whole being.

When he was gone, I sat down on the living room couch and cried (with Laurie holding me) with the same intensity I had when I'd realized my mother was dying and would not be leaving U.C.L.A. Medical Center. The uncontrollable sobs would not stop—no matter what I told myself, no matter how I rationalized. Not only was my heart broken, but my spirit was as well.

I couldn't put any pieces of the gigantic puzzle together. I thought my grief that day would surely kill me, and I remembered the scripture, "This sickness shall not end in death." But I wished it would.

Two days later I had to respond to some correspondence from my dear friend, Dr. James Dobson. I didn't plan to say anything about my confrontation with my irregular person. But to my surprise, I added a P.S. and said, "Guess what weird thing my [irregular person] has done now? . . . He's not coming to Rick's wedding because he has a picnic to attend!"

I know now that postscript was God-inspired. Jim *instantly* perceived that my short closing message was the most important statement I'd ever put down on paper. He was so right. Here is a part of the response I received from him:

> Joyce, I am more convinced every day that a great portion of our adult effort is invested in the quest for that which was *unreachable* in childhood.
>
> The more painful the early void, the more we are motivated to fill it later in life. Your irregular person never met the needs that he should have satisfied earlier in your life, and I think you are still hoping he will miraculously become what he has never been. Therefore, he constantly disappoints you—hurts you and rejects you.
>
> I think you will be less vulnerable to pain when you accept

the fact that he cannot, nor will he ever, provide the love and empathy and interest that he should. It is not easy to insulate yourself in this way . . . but it hurts less to expect nothing than to hope in vain.

I would guess that your irregular person's own childhood experiences account for his emotional peculiarities, and can perhaps be viewed as his own unique handicap. If he were blind, you would love him despite his lack of vision. In a sense, he is emotionally "blind." He's blind to your needs. He's unaware of the hurts behind the incidents and the disinterest in your accomplishments, and now Rick's wedding. His handicap makes it impossible for him to perceive your feelings and anticipation. If you can accept him as a man with a permanent handicap—one which was probably caused when *he* was vulnerable—you will shield yourself from the ice pick of his rejection.

I read Jim's letter over and over, and wept with relief. Here was a letter that did not make me sorry I'd risked exposing my deep feelings, nor was it a judgmental tirade. No sermonette with three points on the "virtues of forgiving" was included—just a letter which helped me, for the first time in my life, put on the shoes of my irregular person to see what walking in his world was all about. I found that my friend had peeled back a dark film from my heart, and it forever changed my ability to see and perceive my irregular person's words, actions, and responses. I will always be grateful!

The letter spoke to several areas.

It showed me how futile and wasted was my hope that my irregular person would "miraculously become what he has never been."

A young wife told me, after a seminar on this subject, "For thirty-one years now, I have wet my pillow with my tears every night, wishing for and wanting my daddy's approval. I've never received it. Today, I decided those tears last night are the very *last* I'd waste on what probably can never be! I'm going home to be the woman, the wife, and the mother *God* wants me to be, and I will not squander the tears or one more moment of my life in a fruitless hope."

I wish there were a way on this black-and-white printed page to show you the alive sparkle in her eyes, the loving-yet-firm tone of her voice, and her shoulders and head, which were unbowed. *She was a beautiful woman.* She had decided that the dream goal of her life was nothing more than a misplaced hope, and she left the auditorium healed and free to live the life God had intended for her.

I understood her words and her feelings. It was not too long ago that I remarked to my friend, Jim Smoke, "Isn't it funny? I'm in my forties, but I still long for my irregular person's approval." Jim answered tenderly, "You don't need his approval, Joyce. You need a healing." Well put.

Jim Dobson's letter brought the first blush of healing for me.

Secondly, the next part of the letter gave me a large measure of insight as to what may have made my irregular person irregular in the first place. I had never really thought about his own childhood as being painful, but the closer I looked, and the more I recalled family tales and anecdotes, the closer I got to the truth. Puzzle pieces, out of nowhere, began dropping into place.

Of course, my irregular person had been *severely* handicapped as a child. It made a great deal of sense. Though I did not know the hows, the whys, or the who-did-its of his life, I was sure that *somehow, something* or *someone* had emotionally crippled him!

I will probably never know the exact details and circumstances of my irregular person's childhood, but just understanding that he must have suffered from the rejection syndrome allows *me* to accept the breakdown of his relationship to me.

I need no other evidence or proof. The Holy Spirit speaks

softly and brings alive the words in Isaiah 43, "Remember ye not the former things, neither consider the things of old. Behold, I will do a new thing; now it shall spring forth; shall ye not know it? I will even make a way in the wilderness, and rivers in the desert" (Isa. 43:18–19, KJV).

In Anne Ortlund's excellent book, *Children Are Wet Cement* she says, "Your child is wet cement, and affirmations are the forms to mold him to his future shape."[1] I wonder who gave my irregular person any affirmations when he was a child? I suspect, from what I know of his family, that lots of correction, information, and advice was daily dispensed . . . but affirmations? Few, if any.

Also, Mrs. Ortlund writes, "Why is it important to affirm a child? Because a child who is truly accepted by his parents . . . can grow up learning to accept himself. . . . He'll be able to admit his own failures and weaknesses. He'll be able to forget about himself and love others."[2]

Perhaps the rigid discipline and the lack of any affirmation has done exactly this to my irregular person. He cannot accept himself, so accepting others is an effort in futility. He is unable to admit or ever forgive himself for his failures and weaknesses, so he cannot forget himself. And, though he loves others, he cannot show or express his love.

Realizing this also gave me some clues about my attitude and expectations about my irregular person. It's a little like the old bromide we have all yelled at our children when they were little: *"Why don't you grow up?"* Most four-year-olds are going to always be a couple of years (give or take) *behind* a six-year-old in development and behavior. But sometimes we forget this fact, and we expect more from our children than they are capable of doing. When we do this, we heap undue pressure and put unreal expectations on little heads and hearts that are yet too young.

Often in life we are so hurt and angered by the irregular person we lose all patience and *expect* him or her to act like "grown-ups," or at least to behave in what we feel is a "normal" manner. When they don't, we continue to *expect* them to and begin pulling our hair out with the frustration of it all!

On the other hand, I've never *expected* my dear friend, Mary Korstjens, in the almost twenty years I've known her, to pour *me* a cup of tea, to hold my face in her hands and comfort me when I am in pain, or to ever walk into my living room—nor has anyone else expected these things of Mary. We have all accepted her as she is—paralyzed by polio. Of course accepting her was easy because, in the first place, *she* made it easy, and, second, because she is such a special lady, you become instantly willing to make allowances. Her husband's book about their life together is aptly called *Not a Sometimes Love*,[3] and it gives you many reasons to accept Mary as she is.

But what of the unlovely, unkind, unsympathetic, and certainly insensitive relative in our lives? My friend's letter held the answer to that. We *must* perceive our irregular person as perhaps "permanently handicapped." It is the only avenue to take towards acceptance and healing.

Another dear friend wrote me much later: "I guess the time, a few years ago, when you talked to me about treating my mother-in-law as a sick or handicapped person brought about one of the real changes in my feelings towards her. I *did* learn to quit expecting her to be 'normal,' and I quit expecting her to 'love' me as *my* mother had loved her in-laws."

We have a choice here. We can say this bad relationship is our irregular person's fault—and become as irregular as he or she. Or we can "make allowances," as Paul tells us, for their faults and handicaps. It's up to us.

Besides teaching me that I must not hope in vain, and that I must accept my irregular person without trying to change him, Jim's healing letter, in the last part, dealt with the reality of how impossible it was for my irregular person to see and hear me.

I think that, *even to this day*, my irregular person is completely and totally unaware of his annihilating words and his destructive behavior towards me and others in the family. The more I realized that my irregular person *probably did* love me, but was unable (and even unconsciously was unwilling) to show his love in words or actions, the easier it became to understand him.

Author and friend Virginia Rohrer gave me some answers to the "whys" of irregular people in a brief note. She wrote:

> I'm glad you're dealing with the subject of irregular people in your newest book. It seems to me there are three classifications:
> 1. *Regular irregulars*—those with deficient upbringings.
> 2. *Personality-defect irregulars*—those who are serious misfits in society.
> 3. *Sociopathic irregulars*—those with no feelings, no guilt; who need no help or person, and yet who charm many people. These never get well unless God does a miracle.

Reading Virginia's list, I realized that my irregular person *could* be one of these or a blend of *two*, and that maybe someone could disintegrate into all three. Surely Virginia has called it like it really is.

I added a fourth category just because this one has been verified many times in my research:

> 4. *Mental irregulars*—those with a definite form of mental illness or the aging problem of arteriosclerosis, which affects the brain process.

The sad thing is that very few, if any, on this list of irregulars really *know* what they are like or how disturbing and complicated they have made our lives.

Perhaps you have already read Dr. James Dobson's *What Wives Wish Their Husbands Knew About Women*, but here I want you to transfer something he said about dealing with marriage to the subject of your relationship with your irregular person.

He wrote:

> Change that which can be altered,
> explain that which can be understood,
> teach that which can be learned,
> revise that which can be improved,
> resolve that which can be settled, and
> negotiate that which is open to compromise.[4]

These are powerful life-transforming statements. I don't believe we can attempt them if we have misplaced hopes and hold badly aimed expectations of our irregular person. But, in my own life, the healing began once I chose to see and understand my handicapped and seriously limited irregular person.

Before I close this chapter, I want to go back once more to Joseph.

As we pick up the story, it is thirteen or fourteen years since Joseph's ten irregular brothers conspired to kill him. Joseph, now thirty and prime minister of Egypt, sees his brothers, severely tests them to see if they have changed, and finally tells them *who* he is.

The brothers *have* changed. The years of stricken consciences have been hard on them. They are full of repentance and, as soon as they grasp that this noble lord is really Joseph, their hearts are truly broken.

I have to believe that Joseph could have *never survived* those thirteen or fourteen years without having chosen, early during his trip to Egypt, to trust God. He must have believed and accepted the fact that, for some reason, his brothers' hatred might never cease.

Joseph finally must have come to terms with God and decided that nothing but God could change their relationship. That's what makes Joseph's words so powerful as he weeps and says to his brothers, "You meant evil against me; but God meant it for good" (Gen. 50:20, RSV). Somewhere along the line, he accepted his brothers as they were—leaving the outcome of their relationship in God's hands.

Notice I did not say Joseph merely *resigned* himself to the annihilating fact that he had ten irregular brothers—I said he *accepted* it.

There are several worlds of difference between *resigning* ourselves to deplorable situations and painful relationships and *accepting* them. No one has stated the difference between resignation and acceptance better than Creath Davis in his book, *Lord If I Ever Needed You It's Now!* I've separated his statements for greater emphasis, but these are his words,

> Resignation is surrender to fate.
>   Acceptance is surrender to God.
> Resignation lies down quietly in an empty universe.
>   Acceptance rises up to meet the God who fills that universe with purpose and destiny.
> Resignation says, "I can't."
>   Acceptance says, "God can."
> Resignation paralyzes the life process.
>   Acceptance releases the process for its greatest creativity.
> Resignation says, "It's all over for me."
>   Acceptance asks, "Now that I'm here, what's next, Lord?"
> Resignation says, "What a waste."
>   Acceptance asks, "In what redemptive way will you use this mess, Lord?"
> Resignation says, "I am alone."
>   Acceptance says, "I belong to you, O God."[5]

Joseph had no illusions about what was required of him in regard to his irregular brothers. Dutiful resignation was *not* an option for him. Joseph chose the best alternative in the world—godly acceptance.

My pastor, Jim Rehnberg, calls this the 50:20 principle. It's where God takes something so bad, even evil, that one human has perpetrated on another human, and turns the *very* acts of hatred and rejection into good, and we, in turn, respond with *acceptance*.

If we are to survive, this is exactly where we need to leave our irregular person—in God's hands.

CHAPTER FOUR

MY SEEMINGLY UNREDEEMABLE CONFRONTATION with my irregular person over my son's wedding date reduced me to tiny, shattered fragments. I was broken not only emotionally, but also physically and spiritually—*especially* spiritually. My faith plunged and poured out of me like water rushes down a large, clean drainpipe.

Hard as it was for me to believe, my irregular person had taken a stranglehold grip on the tree of Christian faith which, up to the moment, had been flourishing in my life. He'd shaken the tree violently, jarred it loose from the soil, and yanked it up, roots and all.

Satan was delighted. And he took enormous pleasure in pointing out that the leaves of my little tree were all gone, that my roots had been exposed to light and air, and that my tree of faith was gasping out its last breath. I almost bought the lie. But, while Satan was convincingly strong, the Lord assured me in my quiet time with Him that *He* was omnipotent and vastly more powerful. I was to wait on the Lord, and the fourth chapter of Psalms, verses three through five, became the rock I found. I held onto it with all my might:

Mark this well: The Lord has set apart the redeemed for himself. Therefore he will listen to me and answer when I call to him. Stand before the Lord in awe, and do not sin against him. Lie quietly upon your bed in silent meditation. Put your trust in the Lord, and offer him pleasing sacrifices. (TLB).

In the immediate days that followed, the Lord used my violent disagreement with my irregular person to produce Dr. Dobson's letter. That letter helped restore my sanity and faith, and my restored faith brought me to the point of taking action.

Also, I realized that:

1. *Spiritually* I now knew the nature of my problem. It was not buried away, but was up on the table in plain sight. And, while I had much to learn about the everyday dealing and coping with irregular people, I was certain that, by God's amazing grace, I'd survive! A tiny healing had begun.

2. *Emotionally* and humanly speaking, if I didn't see my irregular person for a hundred years or more, it would still be too soon. (I knew that was a rotten attitude, but I embraced it anyway.)

3. *Realistically*, I suddenly remembered that in a few weeks there was to be a big bridal shower for Teresa and, in all probability, I'd see the wife of my irregular person.

4. *Pessimistically*, I couldn't figure any of this out. If God had used my friend's erudite and illuminating letter to bring healing (and He had), then why did the thought of seeing my irregular person or his wife begin the shattering process all over again, just as I was about to get it all together? The more I thought of that upcoming bridal shower, the more I panicked, cried, and prayed.

My logical, feet-on-the ground, family counsel suggested that I decide, in view of my friend's letter, just who it was that was sick, and who was the healthy one, in this situation.

Naturally, I chose "healthy."

"In that case," they declared, "you know then that, in

order to have any peace over this, you'll have to be the one to apologize and ask forgiveness."

Incredulously I shouted, "*Me* ask forgiveness?"

The Lord answered quietly within me, "Yes . . . you."

When I went to the Scriptures, the Lord directed me to the same four verses in Ephesians which He had used before in a crisis era years ago, just after we'd found Christ. It was the same song and the same verses.

Read them slowly:

> Don't use bad language. Say only what is good and helpful to those you are talking to, and what will give them a blessing (Eph. 4:29, TLB).

I had used the word *damn* certainly not to help or edify my irregular person, but to get him to listen to me. I had my good and sincere reasons for bad language, but this scripture says clearly that I violated a biblical principle. I was wrong in using the word. I *could* apologize for that:

> Don't cause the Holy Spirit sorrow by the way you live. Remember, he is the one who marks you to be present on that day when salvation from sin will be complete (Eph. 4:30, TLB).

I knew instantly that my behavior during that fateful confrontation had decidedly grieved the Holy Spirit. *That* I didn't ever want to do. Jesus had rescued me, forgiven me, saved me, and transformed me like the caterpillar upon emerging from a cocoon is transformed into a butterfly . . . how could I have forgotten the expensive price tag of my salvation?

Quickly I asked the Holy Spirit's forgiveness, and He beautifully granted it, and it felt marvelous.

> Stop being mean [some translations use the word "bitterness" here], bad-tempered and angry. Quarreling, harsh

words, and dislike of others should have no place in your lives (Eph. 4:31, TLB).

In the days following my argument with my irregular person, I could almost smell the stench of pent-up bitterness and meanness that were rattling about in my soul.

Yet in light of this next verse I knew that, as far as I'd ever been able to determine, the only cure for the infectious disease of bitterness is large and frequent doses of forgiveness.

Be kind toward one another, tenderhearted, forgiving one another, even as God has in Christ forgiven you (Eph. 4:32, RSV).

But how, I reasoned, do you forgive a person who has consistently rejected you? How do you even *begin* to work up an apology to someone who has routinely produced such havoc in your life?

I have some pretty strong opinions about the subject of apologizing to anybody—much less to an irregular person. In the first place, I feel the idea that we should write or telephone almost everyone in our little world, from our childhood sweetheart to the lady that sits behind us in choir, with the generalization of, "If I've *ever* done anything to offend you in the last twenty years or so, I'm sorry," is utterly ridiculous. It really blows me away that some people misinterpret the Scriptures to this extent. A general, blanket apology does nothing except to stir up a multitude of questions in the other person's heart about the last twenty years.

Personally, I believe a real, authentic apology is when we go directly to a person (or persons) and say, "Last Tuesday I said such-and-such," or, "On Thursday, I did thus-and-so. I was wrong. I spoke out of ignorance," or, "I had no business doing that," or, "I repeated something that attacked your personhood and I'm sorry! I intend never to do that again. Will you forgive me?"

This kind of apology requires us to face up to the newly created issues in our lives. That helps us keep our forgiveness up to date. A real apology also forces us to admit we were wrong, and we become willing to assume the responsibility for our words or actions. But most of all, this kind of straight apology changes our attitudes and sets our priorities in a different vein so that Ephesians 4:32 can be a reality in our lives.

But, back to my earlier question, how do you forgive the irregular person in your life?

After a seminar on irregular people, a college girl told me that her roommate turned to her while I was talking about "forgiving" and whispered, "Up to this point, I really liked Joyce Landorf, but when she says, 'forgive,' that does it! I don't like her at all, because there is *no way* I can forgive my irregular person for all the cruelty he's laid on me for the past nine months."

The girl's words are very true. There is *no way* she, or anybody in this whole world, can attempt an apology and ask forgiveness of, much less *forgive*, an irregular person. It is not within the realm of *human* ability to forgive someone who countless times has run over you and your personhood with an enormous steam roller.

Notice—I said *human* ability. That's the crux of the matter here. Humans are limited. Only God is not!

Once I finally admitted to the Lord that there was *no way I* could forgive my irregular person, He did what He has done on one or two other occasions in my life. He beautifully assured me that if I was obedient to Him He, the God of my salvation, would do the forgiving bit. He would do it *through me*. But I did have to make a choice.

I could wallow and die in bitterness, and watch as hatred shriveled up my soul's relationship with not only other people but with God as well. Or I could choose to be a channel for God's forgiveness and stand back to watch an incredible miracle take place.

I chose the latter. But it meant opening my life, becoming vulnerable, learning a new lesson in humility, and, on blind faith, taking a giant step in trusting the Lord.

I decided to become willing to be spiritually teachable. However, I found that putting this lesson in practical layman's terms was a horse of a different color and breed!

"I know the Lord will channel His forgiveness through me," I explained quickly, "but, when I see my irregular person's wife at the bridal shower, what in the world do I *say* when I ask forgiveness?"

"It will come to you," I was told.

That was no help, but strangely enough the Lord *did* begin to help me crystalize the right words that I could, in all honesty, say in my own heart. God started the forgiveness flowing.

The day of the bridal shower was beautiful. My friend Bettye's house and her outdoor patio were like her—beautiful, special, and first-class. Teresa was radiant, and the guests were all family and friends, so everyone was enjoying the occasion, each other, and the entire atmosphere.

The only rain that fell on my parade that day was the presence of the very silent and somber wife of my irregular person. She had arrived late and stayed far across the room from me. I had no opportunity to talk with her until after the luncheon and opening of gifts, so I had a good long time to rehash and rehearse my speech. I felt a small spark of confidence kindling inside of me, assuring me that God *could* channel the apology and bring real forgiveness.

I knew that what I was going to say was exactly what the Lord expected me to say, so I told the acids which wanted desperately to build up in my stomach that soon, very soon, this whole mess would right itself. I'd ask forgiveness.

She'd grant it. Then she'd ask my forgiveness, and later my irregular person would phone or write, saying he was sorry, too. It was all so neat and tidy, or so I thought.

Finally, just before she left, I hugged her and said, "I have been very disturbed about the events of our last visit." Then I apologized for the manner in which I acted, for the language I used, and told her I was just generally sorry for the way the whole confrontation went. "Will you forgive me?" I asked, "And will you talk to [my irregular person] and ask him to forgive me, too, for the way I talked to him?"

Her face lit up, she hugged me genuinely and warmly, and said, three times, "I forgive you, I forgive you, I forgive you." Then she assured me that she would relay the message to her husband and that it would make him feel better, especially in view of the fact that he had been physically ill because of me and my words. After she hugged me again, she said her good-byes and was gone.

For a long time I stood there on the same spot in Bettye's living room. It was so puzzling. I'd been listened to, hugged, farewelled—and had not heard anything that sounded remotely like, "Oh, Joyce, *I'm* sorry too. . . . Will you forgive *us?*"

I was too green, at the time, in understanding or handling irregular people to know that they rarely apologize or take any responsibility for their part in an argument, conflict, or disagreement.

It dawned on me, while I was still in Bettye's living room, that I'd just been given an excellent lesson in obedience. I had done what the Lord *told* me to do, and He had done as He promised: He had let His forgiveness flow *through* me. But it began to dawn on me that the Lord had never *guaranteed* the other party would feel the same way as I did, or that apologies would be *exchanged*.

Yet I can't emphasize enough how peaceful you can feel

after you have obeyed the Lord. I came away from Teresa's bridal shower at rest with the Lord. The matter was not miraculously all cleared up, resolved, or squared away (they were still *not* coming to the wedding), but I'd done what I knew was the *right* thing to do. God had passed a genuine and real apology through me, and it had freed me to join in on all the plans for the wedding, to make my gown, and to be the smiling mother of the groom.

This matter of forgiving others, especially our irregular person, is truly an insurmountable mountain if we try the climb on our own. I can understand if right now you are shaking your head "no" about forgiveness, or exclaiming, "That's easy for *you* to say." Or perhaps you feel as this woman did when she wrote: "Joyce, you don't know *my* irregular person. I can never, in the whole world, forgive her. And certainly, if I could forgive her, I'll never forget the awful things she's done."

However, remember, I am not asking or suggesting that you forgive and forget in your own strength. *I know* for a fact that it *can't be done*.

I do not find it necessary to fill this book with detailed illustrations of my irregular person's words and behavior, or of his abandonment and rejection of others and myself (even though that would add a certain strength and credibility to my claims of being so hurt). But whether your irregular person is worse than, far more terrible than, less irregular than, or just like mine is not the point. The heart of the matter is that the pain of the ice pick of their rejection (as Jim Dobson called it in his letter) has been—and is—*all too real*. Given years to develop, it will eventually take deadly aim at you and me and will kill us with bitterness and hatred.

Forgiving our irregular people for all the things which have hurt us so (whether they return our forgiveness or not) has got to take place if we are to live without bitterness. But we *cannot* do it on our own. Only God can—through us. Apologizing and forgiving and laying it to rest are only possible as we allow God to do it.

A woman who understands this concept of forgiveness wrote,

Dear Joyce,
You said that God will not heal my bitterness. I agree—I found that to be true in my own experience with my irregular person.

But healing came in my life and in my relationship with my irregular person after *I asked the Lord to make me willing* to forgive. I told the Lord I was willing for Him to make me willing.

It was one year later that I came to the point in my life where I could say within myself that I forgave her, and another six months to be able to love her freely—no strings, no hesitations. I had finally accepted her for who *she* was, and I was released of the years of tension and pain.

Another letter on this subject of forgiveness was handed to me at the end of one of my seminars. This woman was about to venture out in the direction of God's channeling. It reads,

My irregular person is my dear pastor husband. I relate to you and your experiences . . . not quite as severe . . . but oh, so hard to take.

He never gives gifts, even at Christmas. Never a card, no words of appreciation, no thanks . . . but he is so good, kind, and sweet to our church family. He always has time for the church and congregation, but no time for me and, in the past, no time for our sons.

I'm going home to work on the resentments I have, but I thank you for sharing.

You have ministered to my hurts today. Thank you.

This pastor's wife had come to the point of knowing she had to choose to take action if she was to survive.

78

Another letter writer speaks of a woman friend:

I have a dear friend who, for forty years, had a husband as her irregular person. She came finally to the point where she told God she had no love for her husband. Then she asked the Lord each day to give her a small healing and some ability to love her husband each minute of the day, if that was possible.

Over a period of time, she gradually won him. He changed, and now, in only five years, he has really changed. He is very sensitive to *her* needs and they are very close.

Nothing in that couple's lives *changed them* over a forty-year marriage except that the wife gave up and asked God to love and forgive *through* her. This isn't an instant miracle we sometimes see performed by some faith healer on TV. But it is a miracle nevertheless! God was truly glorified by this woman's teachable spirit. Her willingness to be used as a channel of God and her submissive spirit to God's timing eventually healed that marriage.

Forgiveness is very costly, even humbling, and seems to take forever, but it is often the price of a good relationship.

My mother had a couple of irregular relationships in her life that I was aware of, but I did not see how painful one was until the year she died.

One of the irregular people in my mother's life was her younger sister, my favorite Aunt Grace. They dearly loved each other and were very close *except* on one thing . . . Christianity. On that subject, my mother and Grace were billions of worlds apart, and they had many noisy and lengthy arguments over it.

Two months before my mother died, we had a Fourth of July family reunion at my parent's home. My aunt and uncle and several of their older children were there. We were all outside after Sunday lunch, enjoying the patio and swimming pool.

Later that afternoon, my sister, Marilyn, came bouncing

out of the pool and asked what time it was. Mother said, "Five-thirty," and Marilyn grabbed a towel, hurriedly dried off, and ran for the back door, explaining she had to get ready for the six-o'clock youth group at our church.

Marilyn didn't even make it to the door before my Aunt Grace launched into an explosion of words. She accused my mother of ramming Christianity and church attendance down our throats, and of ruining Marilyn, myself, and my brother as people with her fanatical emphasis on religion. On she went, and she got louder with each sentence. (Hungarians always give an argument all the steam they've got.)

My mother, who was in the advanced stages of breast cancer, did not have the strength to yell back, so she responded quietly, "No, I don't think I've ever *forced* Marilyn to go to church. She just loves it."

My aunt went on and on, and when she turned to make some other remarks to one of her children, my mother slipped into the house. As soon as I could, I broke away from the group and found my mother, head in her arms, crying at the kitchen table. I had never seen her so distraught. "Is it the pain, Mother, or is it Aunt Grace?" I asked.

"It's her," she sobbed. "I can't understand how she could be so hateful!" Mother looked up at me, "Have I ever pushed you into the Christian life or rammed the Lord down your throat?"

Of course she hadn't. I remember feeling this whole thing—the cancer and now my aunt's accusations—was so unfair. As Pastor Charles Swindoll says, "Life bites," and I found life particularly biting that day.

I cried with my mother, but the lesson I was about to learn from the Lord about forgiving the irregular person was marvelous.

A month later my mother was hospitalized for the last time. My aunt and grandmother were visiting back east, and by the time they returned it was late August. One trip to the hospital told Grace that her sister, Marion, didn't have too much time.

During one of those last visits, my aunt noticed my mother's dry hands, and very tenderly she began to rub lotion into her skin. After she finished Mother's hands, she uncovered her feet and gently massaged them as well. My mother's dark brown eyes took this all in. She made her own mental observations, but stayed very quiet.

After my aunt left that day, Mother immediately found her voice and asked me why Grace had been so tender in words and so gentle in massaging her hands and feet. I shrugged it off by saying, "Aunt Grace knew there isn't much time left for you—"

I think this was the occasion my mother opened her hurting heart and chose to allow God's forgiveness to flow through her. I could almost see her forgiving Grace for all the hurts she had inflicted. I can't be sure about that, but I do know it was that moment when my mother made me promise I'd always pray for Aunt Grace's salvation. Mother made me promise I'd pray, too, for my uncle and cousins, even if there was a divorce or any kind of a disaster in their lives. I was to pray for each one by name and, furthermore, I was to *never* stop until they all found the Lord. Her last words to me on this subject were, "Grace must not die alone, without God . . . without Him."

My mother died September 22, 1966, and I kept my promise about my aunt and her family.

In one way, because I loved Aunt Grace so much, it was an easy promise to keep. But, in another way, it was very difficult. For, in the next ten years after Mother's death, one thing after another happened to my aunt and her family. She and my uncle, surprisingly, *did* get a divorce; their two older sons married and divorced; illness and unemployment plagued the family. They just seemed to deteriorate before our eyes, and the thought of them ever finding the Lord, much less being transformed, grew *very* remote.

Struggling with this, I still kept my promise, but I didn't like the odds.

Then, just a little less than four years ago at this writing, Grace's oldest son accepted the Lord, after a whole night's talk with another cousin who had just become a Christian himself—then another son, a daughter-in-law, and a daughter found the Lord. Salvation just poured into that family, and it was as contagious as chicken pox.

Aunt Grace sat and listened one night as her son, my cousin, excitedly shared his absolutely exuberant testimony and transformation with our whole family. His handsome face, and the faces of his brother, sister-in-law, and sister were just positively radiant as they shared. My aunt smiled, but said very little. In fact, as her son drove her the many miles back to her home, it appeared to him that she was deep in thought. She seemed touched by her children's newly found faith, but kept her thoughts to herself. For once there was no rebuttal or comment from her.

A month later, Grace had a massive heart attack. The doctors discovered that her heart was too diseased even for surgery. On the first day after she gained consciousness in the intensive care unit, she saw a young man standing by her bed. She thought he was a doctor. When he smiled, though, she told him he looked like her nephew, Rick (my son), and added, "He's a Christian." The young man, not a doctor but an intern in the hospital chaplains' organization, replied, "So am I."

"Do you read religious books?" my aunt asked.

"Yes."

"Have you read any of Joyce Landorf's?"

"Of course," he answered, and then explained. "In order to go through the chaplains' course, *Mourning Song* is required reading."

Then Grace said, "She's my niece, and *she's* a Christian."

This beautiful young man did some fast calculating and decided that if she said "Rick and Joyce" were Christians, but never said *she* was—then she probably was not. So he decided to love her into the kingdom of God. He did not talk to her of the Lord (she already knew the finer details of Christianity), but held her hand in his daily visits, answered questions she had about the tubes and treatment, and became an ambassador of Christ and a loving friend to her.

Three weeks later, she was about to be released to go home. And all by herself, in her hospital room she asked Christ to come into her life.

Her first prayer to the Lord, after she asked His forgiveness, was what should she do about her ex-husband? The Lord told her to call him up and ask him if he would like to remarry her. She did, and he said yes!

Although she was still very ill, a month after her release from the hospital my aunt and uncle and their family came to our daughter Laurie's wedding. I'd not seen Aunt Grace since her heart attack and her conversion, so I was not prepared in the least for the incredible transformation and her unmistakable glow of joy.

There were over six hundred people crowded around in the church patio for the reception and the receiving line, but I only really saw Grace. Actually, she was so vibrant and beautiful you couldn't miss her.

She threw her arms around me and *shouted*, "Oh, Joyce, honey, I asked Jesus into my heart and He came. He *really* came. I love Him so much!" This was the same woman who had from day one severely criticized my mother's faith and who now was *shouting* about loving Jesus. I could hardly believe my ears. Immediately I thought of my mother.

"Auntie, my mother must have gone hysterical and turned cartwheels in Heaven when you accepted the Lord!"

Grace's piercing brown eyes instantly bored into me. "Joyce," she said, lowering her voice a bit, "your mother was *there*—in my room, by the end of my bed, when I asked Jesus in." Then she went on to explain. "I looked over at her. Your mother was smiling, and she looked so beautiful. I said, 'Marion, will you forgive me for all the hateful things I've said to you all during your life?'

"Then, Joyce," my aunt continued, "your mother smiled and said, 'I've already forgiven you, honey. . . . You've been forgiven for years.'"

Both Grace and I were oblivious for the moment to the place, the people, and the wedding that brought us together. Then, as the tears streamed down her face and mine, she said, "I asked your mother why I had to be fifty-six years old . . . why had it taken so long to find Jesus? I'd known *about* Him all those years. Why did I fight so long against Him?

"Your mother smiled again and answered so sweetly, 'It doesn't matter *why* now . . . you're home safe.'"

Two months after Laurie's wedding, my uncle turned his life over to Christ. Our hearts soared with joy. Then, five months later, almost in an instant, my Aunt Grace went home to be with Jesus, her newly found Savior.

I could have turned green with envy. I wish I could have seen them—the Lord, my mother, my aunt, and my grandparents—all of them rejoicing. I'll bet they had one smashing reunion party! It was probably very Hungarian and very loud!

The point of this whole story is simply to say that my mother, Marion Miller, had, in the year of 1966, faced the fact that she could not forgive, forget, or accept her sister's tongue lashings, so she asked God to do it *for* and *through* her. The Lord granted her request. And isn't it interesting that the first sign of her spirit's recovery—even as she lay dying—was her plea to me to promise I'd always pray for the very person that had hurt her so?

It proved to be another important lesson.

True forgiveness not only cleans and heals a heart of bitterness, but frees it to be a *giving* heart as well.

Before I close this chapter, I have to talk about another dimension of forgiveness. I must admit that for a long time I did not believe the old cliché, "forgive and forget." I knew by personal experience and was beginning to understand this concept of God forgiving through us. But *forget?* How would that ever be possible? How could we ever erase or forget painful incidences or destructive words once they were established in our conscious or subconscious minds? For years this has puzzled me. Then, because God is so good, He gave my dear friend, Charles Swindoll, *the* most sensible insight on the subject of forgetting I've ever read.

In his book, *Improving Your Serve*,[1] Chuck asks the same question I've asked myself so many times: "Can our minds actually allow us to forget?" Then he explained that he did not refer to forgetting in the technical or literal sense, because we really never forget anything. Rather, he wrote, forgetting, in a godly way means three things:

1. Refusing to keep score (1 Cor. 13:5),
2. Being bigger than any offense (Ps. 119:165),
3. Harboring no judgmental attitude (Matt. 7:1–5).

I hope these brief words will encourage you to read Chuck's whole book. So, without stealing his thunder, let me say that at the end of his magnificent chapter on "The Servant as a Forgetter" he writes: "But forgetting is something shared with no other person. It's a solo flight. And all the rewards are postponed until eternity . . . but how great they will be on that day! Forgetting requires the servant to think correctly . . . which means our full focus must be on the Lord and not on humanity. By God's great grace, it can happen."

So, in the end, forgetting is accomplished just as forgiving is—by understanding we cannot do either one in our own strength, only in the Lord's!

Now, when I remember the horrible pain of that day when my irregular person and his wife wouldn't agree to attend Rick's wedding (and I do remember the day—the words and even the looks), I realize, because I am allowing God to supervise the erasing of that particular memory tape, that He lets me remember *without a need to get even.* He allows me to view my irregular person's words as no big crime, and He lets me remember it all without a judgmental or critical spirit. So, when I remember the words of that day through God's eyes, I am not pierced and wounded all over again, but am able to see Paul's Romans 8:28 and God's lovely hand at work in my life.

Oh, yes, by the way. Two weeks after Teresa's bridal shower, I got a letter from my irregular person. He wrote that, since I had apologized for my terrible behavior and language, they had decided to come to the wedding.

I did not find the letter particularly amusing, then. But I do now! God's brand of forgiving and forgetting *must* be at work within me. Yippee! (Or, to be more spiritually precise—Praise the Lord!)

I close this chapter with a rather long letter written by a young woman who is realistically setting about to cope with, accept, and forgive her irregular mother. I'm including the entire letter with the hope that it speaks to your heart as it did mine:

Dear Mrs. Landorf,

You gave of yourself completely during your talk at Jesus Northwest. You became transparent, and, though you couldn't even see the faces of the lives you were touching, you opened yourself up, became vulnerable, and shared a very personal hurt in hopes that it would help someone else. I want to thank you for your obedience. It takes a great deal of courage and sensitivity to do what you've done, and I thought you might like to know you hit home!

I was one of the faces way up the hill amidst the frisbees and crying babies. But, as you began to speak, those all faded away, and it was just you and me sharing a cup of coffee over the kitchen table.

Up until that point Jesus Northwest had been a relaxing vacation, but most of the ministry had been aimed at the "baby Christians." My husband had been challenged by the morning speaker, but I "had it all together in the Lord" and was just in neutral, coasting along. Then you quietly walked into my peace with a pair of wire cutters and proceeded to snip open the barbed wire fence I'd built around thirty-six years of hurt the irregular person in my life—my mother—had caused.

It is a very weird experience to walk across the fairgrounds with your insides spilling out, tears welling over the rims of your eyes, and the rest of the world is exactly the same! They all proceed on normally—it's like being part of a silent film. Where do you go to get it back together? Then I remembered you were going to be in the Book Area. Thank you for your sweet, understanding spirit. I know you would have ministered to me on the spot, but I was bleeding too badly and needed space and time for the Spirit to stitch me up again. But, I did want your address so I could write you this thank-you letter and also to encourage you in some small way, I hope.

The Lord has been helping me "face up to," "deal with," "accept," and "forgive" my mother. This has been an ongoing process now for the last four years. I realized she was handicapped (I love that term, "irregular") and totally incapable of loving me—my brothers, yes, but not me! And I'd deal with it, forgive, get back up and try again. Every time she'd talk to me she'd spew garbage out of her mouth. It is as if she is a parasite and she gets her bimonthly feedings by dumping all over me twice a month. I'd tell my Christian sisters what she'd say, and it was so foreign to anything they'd ever experienced they couldn't relate or minister to my broken spirit.

I can't tell you how many hours I'd spent in prayer over this matter. The last month or so it has been building to a head. So when you began to speak and share your hurts that are so identical to mine in many ways it really blew me away. I knew I wasn't the only one who'd ever been rejected, but no one else had ever verbalized it before. There is such a release in knowing you aren't alone—the only one! I knew Jesus had been rejected and all the "right" Scriptures to quote. I knew all the correct words to say to forgive my mother. I'd done it all, laid it all on the altar. And, even so, she'd still slay all my self-confidence with one caustic word from her tongue. Why, if I'd followed all the "Christian Ground Rules," did it still hurt so?

You described it so well at the end of your talk. Outwardly I'm coping well, but internally I'm bleeding to death. I have had the same pattern of pain and ill-health as you described—doctors, surgeries, the whole bit. I'm not in a wheel chair, as they said I'd be, but my knee and back are still my weak areas, and when I'm under stress the pain begins. But, I KNOW in my spirit—deep down in that knowing place—God is healing me.

Also I found it interesting that you said your irregular person used to put you down for your sensitivity to others. My mother does the same thing. It was a weakness to her, and, because I was weak and not "tough" like she is—she doesn't even need a God, she can do it by herself, so what's the matter with me—I never measured up and wasn't worth loving. (I praise God every day I'm not like her!) Could it be that though our sensitivity is a gift that God uses, it is a threat to our irregular persons because they don't have it, can't understand it, and just plain see it as a flaw or weakness? This irritates them that we aren't just like they are. They are "perfect," so the fact we aren't carbon copies and don't see, think, agree with them in all ways is a rejection of them—in their eyes. They are incapable of accepting differences in people—they are intolerant, rigid, inflexible, strong-willed, highly opinionated, unloving people. And, God made them and He loves them and I must too! Therein lies the rub—!!!

Be at peace for me. God is in control, and when I heard you speak, it was as if He said, "See, I do hear your prayers, and together we'll see it through." But it sure was pleasant and a real blessing to have "that cup of coffee" with you on that July afternoon. (Wait a minute—scratch the word "pleasant." It hurt—-but I grew.) Sharing experiences makes the burden lighter.

Your sister in Christ.

I sense this woman will land on her feet, even though her years of failing have been so excruciating. Her desire to be God's woman is evident, and I have to believe our God, who keeps all the records straight, will see her through. We can count on it!

CHAPTER FIVE

I WISH I COULD SAY that in the year after Rick's wedding three wonderful things began to happen:

1. I wish I could say that allowing God's forgiveness to flow *through* me brought an end to the emotional war of hurt and angry feelings within me.

2. I wish I could say that, because God dramatically changed *my* attitude, forgiveness and change automatically covered my irregular person, and that he began to respond to God's touch.

3. Most of all, though, I wish I could say that, with Dr. Dobson's letter and the insights on forgiveness I received from the Lord, I immediately developed into a mature Christian woman, capable of handling and coping with any emotionally complicated relationship.

However, what I wish I could say now and what really happened then are a couple of light years apart.

First of all, I was to learn that, over the next years, my irregular person would present me with unlimited opportunities to call upon the Lord to restore again and again the forgiveness in my own life. Our relationship had taken many years to become this painful, and to expect the Angry Feelings Department in my emotional life to simply melt away was highly unrealistic.

Second, it slowly dawned on me, after a few more years of highly frustrating encounters, that my irregular person would not, or could not, ever change—unless God changed him. Earlier I had accepted my irregular person as he was, but always there had been the hope that he would be different, or that *I* would make him different, or that maybe in time he would at least mellow. But gradually I was able to see that his own hurts were so ingrained within him that the chances of his dealing with them or changing were very slim. (Let me hasten to say this *may not* be the way God deals with your irregular person; I am only telling you how things were in my case.)

Most painful of all was the knowledge that even though I had opened this can of worms, faced the conflict, educated myself about my irregular person's particular handicap, and readily dealt with forgiveness and forgetting—I still had to go on dealing with my frustration and personal hurt. My expectations that these would go away had been unreasonably high.

I did experience a growing level of spiritual maturity through this whole episode, and since the Holy Spirit had channeled forgiveness through me, I certainly felt I could handle most anything. Almost smugly, I said, "Let my irregular person throw any curve ball he wants to—I can catch it and run with it!" Right?

Wrong.

As is my nature, I was taking over and not allowing God to work or forgive through me. In addition, although I had begun dealing with my irregular person on a spiritual level, I had not dealt with him on an emotional level. I had overlooked and denied my own long-pent-up feelings, and now they refused to be kept down.

Anger was the emotion which seemed to override all others in me when it came to my irregular person. I began to notice that, whenever I would have a conversation with him on the phone or at Christmas or family get-togethers, I would end up getting very angry. I was appalled at the vehemence of my feelings; I wondered what this anger and hostility were doing in a nice Christian lady like me—especially one who had *forgiven* the person who was causing all the anger!

I have since learned that this happens to a lot of people who must deal with an irregular person. One woman wrote me a fairly long letter, which I've excerpted here:

> My irregular person has drained the well dry. There is no love left. I pray for her every day. Your tape on "God's Waiting Room" fit my situation, also, for I have been in this particular waiting room for more years than I can count. God cannot help her, because she will not let Him into her heart, so I can't be helped in this situation, only by His strength. I have a family to raise, and a godly Christian man to love and care for, and I know I must remain strong and not let this thing win over and get me down.

Then, at the end of her letter, she aptly describes this emotion which troubles so many of us as we try to cope:

> Thank you for listening, Joyce. I think this letter has been a type of therapy for me—but I think my real problem is that I am filled with deep anger and do not know how to express it. This would be good to cover in your book.
>
> I am angry that I cannot be happy in my family circle—that one person can try to ruin my life—and that my very own mother can turn on me instead of loving me. I would imagine that is a feeling many of us with irregular people have in common.

How right she is. Anger *is* a feeling many of us have in common . . . and somehow just facing it is a start in the right direction.

Dr. Dwight L. Carlson is an M.D., a practicing psychiatrist. I wish his book, *Overcoming Hurts and Anger*, had been published a long time ago; I would have been terribly relieved to have read his comments about conflict being both normal and inevitable. Also, I would have been comforted by these words: "It is simply a fact of life that the people who are closest to you are the people with whom you are most likely to get angry. . . . Expect it because it is, in fact, normal; it is part of life. . . ."[1]

The first time my own anger exploded during a phone call from my irregular person, I was genuinely shocked at my unspiritual behavior. How could this be? Here I was, feeling furious, and the adrenaline was pumping through my veins with the force of a thousand-pound thrust. So there I stood, shaking with rage, and the fruit of the Spirit called self-control evaporating fast! I found myself hotly defending my position, and saying things I knew I'd deeply regret later on.

This happened again and again. *Why can't I have a loving conversation with this man?* I wondered. I loved him, I'd accepted him, and God was beautifully forgiving him through me. So why did every encounter turn into an insane rush down a dead-end alley? The emotional stress of these conversations was mounting with alarming speed.

About that time I read a book by a Christian counselor who advocated loving confrontation as a way of healing broken family relationships. He implied that one just had to call, make a date to talk, then go follow through—see the other person and quietly discuss old hurts. Soon both parties would see it all clearly, forgiveness would come, and the old established walls of rejection would come tumbling down.

I wanted to yell, "Are you kidding?" I felt that the fairy tale where the frog turns into a prince after the princess kisses him has a lot more credibility than the simplistic answer of merely talking to someone, soothing their feelings, and making everything right.

However, as I continued to read books and articles by psychologists and psychiatrists, Christian and secular, all of whom talk about easing the anger out of our lives by confrontation, I began to understand and *believe* in its extraordinary therapeutic value. Besides, as I thought about it and studied the Scriptures, I began to realize that confrontation is clearly God's method of handling the anger (call it hurts, frustrations, or whatever) that comes from our painful relationships.

Read Jesus' words in Matthew:

> "Under the laws of Moses the rule was, 'If you kill, you must die.' But I have added to that rule, and tell you that if you are only angry, even in your own home, you are in danger of judgment! If you call your friend an idiot, you are in danger of being brought before the court. And if you curse him, you are in danger of the fires of hell.
>
> "So if you are standing before the altar in the Temple, offering a sacrifice to God, and suddenly remember that a friend has something against you, leave your sacrifice there beside the altar and go and apologize and be reconciled to him, and then come and offer your sacrifice to God" (Matt. 5:21–24, TLB).

This passage of Scripture is precious to me because our Lord assumes that *some* relations with other people will churn my soul in anger. (Actually, the Lord knows that the thing which angers me most is when someone *devaluates* my personal worth.) He tells me the dangers of letting my angry feelings consume or control my life. The Lord even knows that, at some point in time, I may call my irregular person an idiot (or worse), and again He points out the dangers. I cannot let my feelings rule my life . . . they are too terribly unpredictable. I have to let the spiritual *facts* of my life rule—but, oh, how easy it is to forget the facts and concentrate on the feelings!

There must be a concerted effort on my part to choose the how, when, and intensity of my expressions of anger. It blesses me that God knows I'll have feelings of anger—after all, He did create them. And carefully He tells me to "be angry but sin not." When my anger is running ram-

pant, then I am in great danger of hurting s
that's the sin. Not anger, but venting my anger in such a
way that it damages others.

Then, in that same passage of Scripture, Jesus goes on to
the matter of confrontation. He urges me, before I proceed
in living the Christian life one more day, to confront the
other person, apologize for my own actions, and then go
back to the Temple to worship and serve our Lord. He does
not give me a guarantee that my irregular person will magically, mysteriously, and miraculously be transformed—
only that I will be in right standing with God.

So, as I see it, God's Word directs us to the following way
of dealing with our anger toward our irregular person:

—allowing forgiveness to flow through us from God,

—choosing to ask the Holy Spirit to control the venting
of our anger, and

—confronting in love, no matter what results.

That's truth—not man's opinions, judgments, or solutions—but God's truth. These are the methods of good spiritual, emotional, and mental health, and I believe in them
with all my heart.

According to Dr. Carlson, here is the true definition of a
loving Christian confrontation: "Confronting the other person should not be construed as a sign of hostility; rather, it
indicates that you care enough about that person to work
out the problems in the relationship, no matter how painful
the process may be. . . . Expressing one's deepest feelings
can in fact be a very cleansing experience, one in which love
and respect shared between the two people is usually
strengthened."[2]

David Augsburger, in his book, *Caring Enough to Confront*,[3] lays down seven *before*-requirements for confronting. He writes (the italics are mine):

1. A context of *caring* must come *before* confrontation.
2. A sense of *support* must be present *before* criticism.

3. An experience of *empathy* must *precede* evaluation.
4. A basis of *trust* must be laid *before* one risks advising.
5. A floor of *affirmation* must undergird any assertiveness.
6. A gift of *understanding* opens the way to disagreeing.
7. An *awareness* of love sets us free to level with each other.

This is the kind of guide rule for authentic, loving confrontation that really works. I can run with it. It's especially true if I am talking about a loving confrontation with a cherished loved one, or a family member who is *regular.*

But what about my irregular person? That is where I run into a snag.

It is true that I believe wholeheartedly in confrontation as a way of healing broken, angry relationships. I believe this is what God's Word teaches, I respect many of the authorities I have read who advocate confrontation, and I have experienced its healing power myself in other relationships. But it is also true that my attempts at confrontation with my irregular person did not work out that way!

Over and over again, when the confrontation was with my irregular person, few, if any, of those seven guidelines were put into practice, and so the situation would harden into an unsolvable mess. I would be left with anger and bloody, raw, hurt feelings, wondering what in the world was going on.

Then slowly, with the Lord's insight, I learned after many aborted attempts at confrontation that, while the most mentally and emotionally healthy thing in the world was to have a loving confrontation, my irregular person wanted no part of it! His handicap rendered him quite clearly incapable of dealing with confrontations, no matter how loving I intended them to be.

I had no way of understanding it then, but I now know that my irregular person had never examined or faced up to the enormous stockpile of anger in his own life, simply because he could not face up to any personal problem. And his philosophy seemed to be that Christians don't have anger—although those of us who know him well saw his inner rage reflected in his sharp criticisms of other people, his obvious jealousy of others in his profession, and his deeply negative view of some people and of life in general.

Time after time, in confronting him, I'd state my case, share my inner hurts, and ask what *we* could do about this. He would laugh, pat me on the shoulder, and deny there *was* a problem! Sometimes he'd say, "Joyce, you don't know all the facts I know." And then he'd add, "I'm right on this. You'll see." But the verbal and nonverbal communication which pierced my inner being with the greatest speed was, "*I* don't have a problem. It's too bad you do."

Irregular people, I now know, can rarely admit that they *just well may be part of the problem.* And you cannot have a confrontation with an irregular person if he or she refuses to be confronted. As I see it, their handicap causes them to deny the reality of a fearfully complicated relationship.

In my case, a loving confrontation may yet work out in the distant future—I don't know God's plans on this. And I do believe my past attempts at such confrontation were the right thing to do. But for now, confrontation with my irregular person serves no purpose except that Satan gets to rejoice about the emotional turmoil of two Christians—one in denial and one in frustration.

So what do we do in situations like these? How do we deal with our angry feelings when attempts at loving confrontation just don't work to solve the problem? Some letters I have received suggest some possible approaches.

A new friend of mine, tired of "no results" confrontations with her mother, wrote, "My mother is my irregular person. She has caused so much pain, so much growth, so much confusion, and it's not over! I found a letter I wrote to her and never sent. It was typed on my old typewriter, so I'd guess it was written about two years ago. . . ."

Here are some excerpts from my friend's letter. While she never mailed it, the writing of it uncovered some of her own deeply buried hurts and was, in itself, extremely therapeutic.

Dear Mother,

You probably are wondering what has been upsetting me lately, and the last time you were here, you informed me that you were not coming over any more. I think we need to talk. First of all, I'd like you to sit down and write out a list of what you'd like in a daughter, and like our relationship to include! Second, I'd like you to think over what has happened between you and me, you and my husband, and you and the children.

I have done both of these things. I have thought what I'd like in a mother, in you, and what your relationships are like with me, and my son, and my daughter. These are my answers.

I would like a mother to be a friend, a listener, and be able to interact on an adult level. Specifically, I'd like you to like me as a person. I would like you to stop manipulating me, applying guilt when convenient, and stop overriding my authority with my children.

I am an adult, have been one for a long time. I am a person who has feelings. I get very tired of you and my sister informing me how things are going to be and constantly reminding me that you and she do not respect me because I'm too easygoing.

I am tired of my son being so hurt by your rejection. He tells his friends and their parents that you do not love him any more. They have come to me because of what he has said. He no longer cares when, or if, you come. This is of your own making.

It seems that you have never been able to read me or see what I'm going through. When I think of conflicts that I used to have with you when I was living at home, they were always non-productive and meant defeat rather than growth. That is all water under the bridge. But what I'm getting at is the fact that it seems you are still treating me as if I'm a child, not an adult, and that my constant striving for adulthood is a threat to you.

I think you need to do a couple of things. I think you need to take a look at who I am! I think you need to decide what you want of me and what kind of a relationship you want with me.

My friends do not take the liberties that you do, and I don't want you to either. Just because you are my mother does not give you the right to put me down, do as you please with my children, and generally disregard how I feel. *If* you looked at me the way others did, you'd love me for who and what I am. You would be thankful for what you have. I think, basically, I'm a very nice person with imperfections like everyone else. Never once have you asked about my business, or how I'm doing. Never once have you shown any interest in what I'm doing.

So, I have decided that the time is now. That we either begin to work at being respectful friends, or the strain of me trying to be loved and recognized will burst, and I will cope by shutting it all out and go on with life. I do not need to be used. I am not masochistic, nor do I need to be mistreated and denied my rights as a human being. You have no special license because you are family. I think of the saying, "Why do we always hurt the ones we love?" and my answer to that is: because we do not feel the freedom to be honest and free when we should be able to. Being too close to a situation takes away freedom that is sometimes necessary for survival.

I have always felt that you did not understand me or my motives. So, I guess you are left with a decision. Either you begin consciously to understand me, or you lose me. I do not have to prove myself to you. I do not have to be anyone but myself. What you want to hear from this, and what you get out of this, is your own doing. You can pout. You can be angry with me. You can resent. You can disown me. But you can also be sorry that it's gone this far. I am. And you can learn, not because it's demanded and expected. I have learned a lot about the word *respect* versus *expect*. When you expect, it's all what comes *from*. Respect, it all comes *to* . . . look the two up in the dictionary. So, here it is, in all its pain and truthfulness. It is yours to do as you see fit.

In another letter, this time to me, the same friend wrote,

. . . I really feel the Lord wants me to heal and to be open to His miracles. And, as for my irregular person, I think one never really gives up *hope* that things will be different.

Oh, how I could identify with you when you said, "Don't let her rain on your parade." I have a lifetime of rained-out parades and sadness, wanting things to be different.

Near the end of this letter, she added,

I was reading, last night, an article from the latest "Family Health Magazine." The article quoted Dr. Siegel, and it applies to me. "If you do things because you love, then you yourself will be healthier. If you do things to *gain* love, then you will get sick." I have personally turned those tables, and am healthier than I ever have been.

Another dear friend now deals with the fact that her irregular person, her mother, is with the Lord. While her mother was alive, loving confrontations were not possible. My friend's letter tells about that and her own emotional progress.

Dearest Joyce,

I have been thinking quite a bit about my mother. Your note came on Monday, the sixteenth, the one-year anniversary of her death. So, let me try to tell you, as best I can, how I feel about her. Here are a few things I've decided:

First, with the passing of time, I've come to realize better that my mom really must have tried to be the best mother she could have been. I just think that she failed, in my eyes, because she did not reach my expectations (hopes, desires) of what I wanted her to be. Within her capacity, I think she was the best mother she was able to be, and had she even realized that I wished for so much more in terms of real communication I think she would have really tried to meet those needs. But our differences were just too great for us to bridge. (I guess what I'm saying is that they seemed so insurmountable that I would die before I tried to tell her, and bridge that gap.)

If any change were to be made, I feel I would have had to have taken the first step, and this I never could pull myself together to do. The thought was just too emotionally devastating to me. I had grown to feel so uncomfortable around her, because I didn't feel I could ever show my true feelings, or hurts, or needs. We just never talked about such things as a family.

I don't want this to sound cruel, but in some ways my hurt is easier to handle now that she's gone to be with the Lord. (And I really think she's there!) In many ways she showed the fruits of the Spirit, as I look back. Just in this one area—where she did not meet me at the need of my emotional insecurity—did she fail to be anything but the type of mother we'd want. She met our physical needs. She never worked outside the home, helped in Girl Scouts, and did all the seemingly right things. I never remember her and my father having a verbal disagreement. They always seemed to be in harmony with one another. But, I'm straying from my point!

Now that she is in heaven, I don't have the constant reminder, every time I go to my parents' home, that my emotional needs aren't being met, nor do I have the guilt that *I* should be the one to try to change things, or that I'm thinking, *She's my mother! How can I feel that way about her?*

Also, I've been trying to absorb the truth that (as much as I don't like it) I *can never* have another mother—someone to meet those needs just like I'd like to see them met. The ache in my throat, or the sting behind my eyelids when I think about this, won't change the fact: I do not have a mother. No one can ever be that mother I long for so!

This void in my life will have to be filled, somehow, by God—as I'm able to see how He would like to heal my hurt in this area. The relationship I so long for with an older woman—like your and Laurie's relationship, or your and

Teresa's—may never be! That's a crushing blow to me. I so long to have a mother-figure to just *love me unconditionally!* Someone who really wants to be with me, and go shopping with me, and help me choose things to spruce up my house on my limited budget—that's what I ache for in my moments of depression and aloneness.

So what happens from here? My common sense tells me that I cannot have that so-wanted relationship with a mother, but I must do all within my ability to be sensitive to my own daughters so they will have every opportunity to open up with me. I want to be the kind of mother I dreamed I could have to my own girls. And that's hard! When you've been brought up in a home where you never talk about anything other than surface things, you never hug, never remember "Laughter in the walls," how do you learn these things that will allow you to change in your own household?

If I had it to put in a nutshell, I guess I'd say: I don't hold my mother at fault for the way she was; I think she did the very best she could. I still, however, mourn for that mother I always wish I'd had, and never will, and I so want to be that special kind of mother to my kids.

Even without a loving confrontation, this special friend of mine has opened her heart to God's healing. She's willing to admit and face the painful voids in her life, and she is coming out with some highly prized, God-given lessons learned. I am close to her, personally, and I've watched the Lord shape her into the woman, wife, and mother *He* had planned for—all along!

Another confrontation-type letter, from a couple I do not know, started out with these words:

> The first time I called my mother-in-law "Mom," I was icily told, "I am not your mother." From then on, I tried very hard to find just what my place was in my husband's parents' home. I found that home to be a very exclusive place.
>
> My husband was welcomed at all times, of course. But I was not received as a member of the family. And so I tried

to make a place of sharing womanly things with my mother-in-law. She would use this time for pumping me for personal information about our private lives. How much did her son make? How much did I spend for groceries? Etc. . . .

Later, in their letter, the husband talked about his mother's terrible relationship with his wife, and he described the irregular-person problem with these words: "This was war. Actual declared war. And it was our family—our marriage—that was under attack."

After a barrage of attacks, this brave young husband wrote, "I knew I couldn't get through to my mother in person. The situation was much too fragile. The right words were too hard to come by. I decided to write her a letter."

Dearest Mother,

I feel certain things still have not been brought to the light. I am writing this letter both as a son and as a husband.

Our love for each other, as mother and son, exists. God made you my mother as surely as He made me your son. But I have left father and mother to cleave to my wife. The Bible says the reason that we were made male and female was to be joined—to become one—to be no more twain, but one flesh. These are the Master's words. So when I left father and mother something new began. A wonderful mystery in God's universe of mysteries. Two had become one. That's a fact, Mother, not a symbol.

If my wife were blind, I would walk as she, not charging across intersections, but carefully and securely guiding her, for I would be her eyes. We are one flesh. You see, whatever she is, or whatever anyone thinks of her, does not alter what God has made. She and I are one.

And so, Mom . . . if she is rejected, then I, too, am rejected. I think you mean well. But your desire is toward me alone. And I don't exist alone anymore. Your desire must be toward us, or not at all.

Mom, this is all tough to deal with in the flesh, but if we

can join together in the Spirit and ask for God's healing, I'm sure that He will help us.

Love, Your son.

To my knowledge this letter did not change the young man's situation with his mother, but look at what happened between him and his wife! She ended their letter to me with these words,

> My husband insisted on reading the letter to me before he mailed it to his mother. I was overwhelmed. Did he really feel that way about me? Was he actually going to mail it? Suddenly our oneness was more than just words.
> And in the weeks and months that followed, my husband took special care to show me that what he wrote was true. And gradually I was free from that vulnerability that made me such easy prey. I was part of him. We were no more twain, but one flesh.

Sometimes family wars go on endlessly and pass from generation to generation. The battles never seem to be won, and minds and hearts grow sick with weariness and depression.

How beautiful that this young man clearly saw his wife fighting for her very existence on the emotional battlefield of her life, and he *joined* her to defend their love and marriage!

One other thought on confrontations is about the gentle support of others. Now, sometimes help from others is almost impossible, but there is nothing that nourishes us more than a husband, wife, child, or relative who not only *sees* our pain, but chooses to go bat for us. How often I wished for someone to go to my Irregular Person, put up their hand and say "Enough already." While having the support of others may not change the war, at least we do not feel as if we are losing our minds or are abandoned in the battle.

One of my dearest friends received a long venomous letter from her father-in-law. She had never, in her twenty-two years of marriage to his son, been accepted by this man.

I read the entire letter, sent so recently, and it was thirty-four paragraphs long (yes, I counted them).

In fairness, I should tell you that I believe it was the father-in-law's attempt at confronting, but because it was written without a shred of love, it failed in every aspect.

There was no affirmation, only one verbal rejection after another. He showed no willingness to take his share of the responsibility for the broken ties. As is typical with irregular people, there were no admissions of guilt on his part, and no apologies were made or offered.

It was thirty-four paragraphs containing a few thinly veiled threats, a great many flat-out hateful statements, a number of twisted lies—and all the paragraphs were covered with a thin, saccharin coating of spiritual judgment. Although this man loves God and has been a pastor for many years, when it comes to his daughter-in-law he is consistently blind, deaf, and venomously verbal.

His letter was one of the most destructive documents I've ever read, and I was not surprised that the enormous stress of the confrontational letter came very close to turning my bright, intellectual, and godly friend certifiably insane. Only God's loving, healing hand reached out—through her man-of-God husband, a Christian counselor, and many friends in the Body of Christ—to keep her emotionally and physically with us.

I encouraged her husband to write his father a letter in response. In the days that followed, the Lord impressed him, too, with the urgency. And so, difficult as it was, he wrote his father.

Here are some excerpts. Wherever he used his wife's name or children's names, or has given specific examples, I have removed them, but this was the essence of his response.

Dad,

They say that time has a way of healing wounds; however, that is not always true. Your letter of last July was both untimely and misdirected.

—*Untimely*, because while my wife and I were on vacation, she had started a letter to you, stating that your family is here in California, and the next few years will hold some very special times with our son's graduation as valedictorian, college graduations, and probably weddings. All of which she wanted you and your wife to be able to share with us. I had nothing to do with her decision to write, inviting you to share in our lives, and also to express her willingness to try and salvage a relationship.

—*Misdirected*, because you have no right to write and attack my wife as you so clearly did. The Bible says that the man is supposed to be the head of the home. You exercised that right. However, you failed to allow me the same privilege. Regardless of what you had to say in it, your letter should have been directed to me. I will not allow you to ever attack my wife again. She never saw your December note which was to remind her that, scripturally, the whole thing now rests on her shoulders.

Rejection is not fun for anyone. To not be wanted, approved of, or good enough is not a very elevating manner for a young bride to enter a relationship with her new in-laws. Dad, I don't even wish to recall the numerous times in the next twenty-two years that you reinforced the idea that you were opposed to our marriage by the way you treated her.

May I quickly state that Mother never ever, in any way, belittled my wife. In fact, she often openly expressed to others what a good wife to me, and mother to the children, she was.

To make matters worse, my in-laws accepted me with open arms, making me always feel that they were glad I was now part of their family. Yet in my own family, according to you, my wife didn't quite meet the expectations.

She has always been, and still is, all I could ever want in a wife and the mother of our children. She has put up with—and gone through with me—much more than you could ever imagine. It would seem that in this day and age of broken marriages you would be grateful for her continual support, encouragement, and comfort to me in meeting my many needs—physical, spiritual, and emotional.

I don't feel your letter was that of a man trying to heal a relationship. I was always taught that it takes two to make a fight, and not once in your letter did you mention any possible guilt or responsibility for anything.

There are many things I would love to be able to go back and do over. You see, I feel a great responsibility for the present problem. I should have, in the early days of our marriage, stepped forward and said, "Dad, when I lived at home, I respected and obeyed you. However, I have left home, married a wife, and she is the most important and special person on this earth to me. If you cannot accept her and treat her kindly at all times, we cannot continue to have a relationship." However, I had never stood up to you before, and I failed to do so then.

You questioned that my wife had prejudiced our sons against you. When your letter arrived, my wife was alone. She opened and read the letter, and it accomplished its task. It destroyed her. Our oldest son came home and found her in tears and completely out of control. He saw the letter lying beside her, picked it up, and read it. When our other son got home, his brother informed him of the circumstances, and later that evening I gave him the letter to read for himself. We do not discuss the matter, thus the boys' feelings and opinions have been their own, whatever they may be.

It is a tragedy when existing circumstances break up a relationship. However, I feel it is impossible to reconcile such a situation unless all parties are willing to bear their responsibility realistically and come together in an attitude of mutual respect and acceptance.

Your son.

This letter, and especially its perceptive last paragraph about how a loving confrontation could take place, spoke so strongly to my own heart. The son respectfully honors his father, yet clearly affirms his own deep love and great respect for his wife. Between the lines I could almost hear

Genesis 2:24: "Therefore shall a man leave his father, and his mother, and shall cleave unto his wife: and they shall be one flesh" (KJV).

All of these letters offer some insight into how to handle anger and other negative emotions in situations when loving confrontation just doesn't work. My friend, Dr. James Dobson, has some other very helpful suggestions:

> Are there other ways of releasing pent-up emotions?
> Yes, including the following.
> —by making the irritation a matter of prayer.
> —by explaining our negative feelings to a mature and understanding third party who can advise and lead.
> —by going to the offender and showing a spirit of love and forgiveness.
> —by understanding that God often permits the most frustrating and agitating events to occur so as to teach us patience and help us grow.
> —by realizing that *no* offense by another person could possibly equal our guilt before God, yet He has forgiven us; are we not obligated to show the same mercy to others?[4]

In all honesty, I haven't got a solid-gold answer on what to do about the anger and frustration that come when a confrontation with an irregular person simply doesn't work. I know that confrontations are very scriptural and psychologically valid, and yet when I tried them in my own life they failed.

In my experience, my anger and bitterness subsided only when I *chose* to accept the situation "as is," to be honest with myself about my feelings and trust the Holy Spirit to help me deal with them constructively. For now, I have settled into a peaceful acceptance that, 99 percent of the time, confrontation is truly the right way to go, but that for me and my irregular person it is highly doubtful that verbal corrections can cure or even ease our interesting predicament. I'm looking forward to what God is going to teach me in this area.

CHAPTER SIX

As YOU'VE ALREADY GUESSED BY NOW, the name of this game is *survival*.

Webster says that to survive means to "remain alive or in existence, as after an event or after the death of another." Under the word *surviving*, Webster says, "remaining alive or in existence as, *surviving* relatives." (Undoubtedly Mr. Webster refers to *dead* relatives, but it occurs to me that the definition could also mean surviving broken or dead family relationships.)

Now, when I say *survive*, I do not by any means suggest a pagan grit-my-teeth, pull-myself-up-by-my-bootstraps, get-through-the-days-as-best-I-can philosophy. Not hardly! That approach is very unrealistic, and eventually becomes so difficult it destroys the will to go on.

As a Christian, when I say survival, I mean *out-living*, out-stretching, and out-distancing the irregular person (or persons) in our lives. I refer to seeking out and choosing God's best ways for a healthy survival both physically, emotionally, and spiritually.

For a moment here, I have to go back to the word *forgiveness*. In chapter four, you'll remember the word forgiveness was used in context with letting *God's* forgiveness flow through us to our irregular person. However, here, the word forgiveness pertains to our survival and refers to our *own*, personal set-apart need for God's forgiveness.

"For crying out loud," I can hear you scornfully muttering, "What do you mean *my need* for forgiveness? I've tried everything I know to love and get along with my irregular person. I haven't done anything but try to *heal* this relationship. My irregular person is the one who needs 'personal' forgiveness, not me!"

I hear what you're saying, but my own experiences, coupled with some God-given insights, have given me a different perspective.

Do you realize that the stressful years of our lives, as we have done battle with our irregular person, are bound to have produced many angry and rebellious attitudes in us? I cannot ignore the times when, especially after a painful clash, I have had very dark thoughts exploding in my mind and heart towards this irregular person who has so terribly wounded me or someone I love. To say I've always handled the hurts and the invisible scars this person has inflicted on me as easily as I turn off a light switch is to lie.

Just today I was talking with a friend of mine who is going through some very deep waters. I sensed that she had arrived at some kind of spiritual conclusions because she was more at peace about her circumstances than I have seen her in months.

As we talked, my friend told me how she recently realized that all of her life she had been consumed with anger toward her irregular father and mother. The anger over the years had somehow boiled over into self-pity and a "poor me" attitude had led her into terrible depths of depression. Complicating that was the fact that both of her parents are now dead. This had only added guilt and regrets to a huge stockpile of self-pity already within her.

When she comprehended how anger had drowned her in a needless sea of self-pity, she began to pray in a totally different direction. She *chose* to *stop* feeling sorry for herself because of her irregular parents, and God honored that decision by giving her the first peace she's had in years. The trial that she is suffering from an agonizing divorce as of this moment is still going on, but my friend has found the *source* of her anguish (anger) and turned it over to the Lord and asked His forgiveness. He has heard and answered. He always will!

When she spoke of her long-time anger, she touched my heart deeply, and I knew what she was saying. For even *admitting* we are angry is often a giant step in beginning the survival process.

My brief chat with my friend today confirmed what I already knew: survival starts with *my* asking God's forgiveness. It means presenting to the Lord the endless times I've struck back, argued, yelled, or camouflaged my anger in some form of frozen silence, bitter sarcasm, scalding criticism, or pious self-pity.

A few years ago I discovered that anger and the behavior it drew out of me not only shredded my soul into little pieces; it also ate away and undermined my ties with the Lord. What I lost because of anger was the very thing I wanted most—a right standing with God!

If I read the Old and the New Testaments correctly, a lost or broken connection with the Lord was the *only* thing that made God's people miserable to the maximum degree. In the case of Samson, the loss of right standing with God caused him to self-destruct. But with David, God used the prophet Nathan to expose the loss of right standing, and David went from that annihilating encounter straight to forgiveness. He didn't pass "Go," collect his two hundred dollars, or anything. Psalm 51 records the depth of David's remorse and the anguished cry of his repentance as does no other chapter in the whole Bible.

God heard that plea and, if you turn back a few chapters to Psalm 32, you will see the pure, unadulterated joy of man forgiven. David is restored and reconciled once more to the God he had sinned against.

Can you see yourself in David? I can see me, a person as miserable as a person can be, going from sin, anger and/or whatever crisis, into this:

"What happiness for those whose guilt has been forgiven! What joys when sins are covered over. What relief for those who have confessed their sins and God has cleared their record" (Psalm 32:1, TLB).

Jason Towner, in his book, *Forgiveness Is For Giving*,[1] speaks about *my* needs on the forgiveness level. He writes at length about this, but here are the highlights of his thoughts:

1. Recognize your need for forgiveness.
2. Recognize the need to be gentle with yourself and with others.
3. Realize we can't cry over spilled milk.
4. Allow God to use your defeats as sandpaper to bring out the grain in your life.
5. Ignore the old photo albums.
6. Make forgiving yourself a full-time commitment.
7. Don't accept a substitute for authentic forgiveness.
8. Let go and let God.

So, here it is . . . if I am going to survive, continue to grow, and live a spiritually, physically, and mentally healthy life, I am going to have to start at the top of Jason's list, with *recognizing my own need for forgiveness*, and go on from there. Like David, I must ask God's forgiveness for *my* angry spirit.

I've had eight, almost nine, years now since the day of my first fatal confrontation with my irregular person, but I can honestly say I've had eight years of forgiving *him*, and the last four years of keeping *my own* forgiveness up to date.

As Jason's sixth point specifies, I've had to make forgiving myself (to keep a right standing with God) a full-time commitment. *But it works.* And by God's surprising outpouring of grace, I'm surviving the battle. The first tiny victory in this war of emotions and nerves came with settling up the forgiveness score with the Lord. I began to think I'd survive—and so I have. So can you!

Second, I had to apply the ancient principle found in

Ephesians 5:20 if survival was to continue to go forward: "Always give thanks for everything to our God and Father in the name of our Lord Jesus Christ" (TLB).

One of the first series of Bible-study lessons I taught out here in the desert where I live was on this subject of irregular people. By the time I finished the last in the series, Marilyn, a friend of mine who knows the identity of my irregular person, slipped up behind me as the women were leaving and whispered, "Joyce, I thank God for your _____." (She named my irregular person.)

Half kidding (or was I?) I turned around and said, "Marilyn, for heaven's sake, why would you want to do a thing like that?"

Now, this lady is quite a beauty, but she never looked more beautiful or radiant than when she smiled and said gently, "Because *without* him, you couldn't begin to know how I'm struggling with my irregular person. You wouldn't have any idea what it's like for me to cope with mine, and I believe you are the woman you are today because of the irregular person in your life!"

I was stunned.

The truth of her words slammed into me.

Without my irregular person, would I understand another friend of mine who is frustrated beyond belief because of her irregular sister?

Without my irregular person, would I sense the hurt of a deep, forever-scarred soul of someone whose father is the epitome of irregularity?

Without my irregular person, would I have ever spoken or written about the trauma an irregular grandma can cause an individual or a family?

Without my irregular person, would I have related very well to you, or been able to bind up your wounds or help heal your bleeding emotional sores? (I hope I have!)

I doubt it very much! And God knew that all along. It was His plan to place into my life the rare opportunity to deal with an irregular person on a first-hand basis. I now am using the lessons learned as a healing source—and not just a healing for me, but for thousands of other fellow sufferers.

Think of it, out of all the people and families you and I could have been born into or been related to, God chose this person, and this family—this mother, this father, this brother, this sister—and all along God knew who we would marry and who would be our in-law relatives.

Isn't it funny how ardently we believe (and quickly say to a nonbeliever) that "God has a wonderful plan for our lives"? I suspect that we are not *really* talking about God's plan for our past heritage, our present family connections or disconnections, but that, rather, we mean strictly a *plan* of salvation for now and for heaven later. Yet, in the eyes of God, can our past be separated from our present and our future? I think not! His plan is all-encompassing. Our birth, childhood, adult life, and all the people around us are God-planned, as surely as the sun rises in the east and sets in the west.

My friend Marilyn put her finger squarely on God's progressive plan for my life when she thanked God for my irregular person. Her statement, however, uncovered the realization in me that never once had I ever considered thanking God for my irregular person, and that thinking led me back to Ephesians 5:20: "Giving thanks always for all things unto God and the father, in the name of our Lord Jesus Christ" (KJV).

Now, lest you think that something was lacking in my theological training or missing from my thousands of hours in church, I hasten to tell you I am *very* familiar with Ephesians 5:20; and, yes, I've read Merlin Carothers' book, *Prison to Praise*. Furthermore, for years I *have tried to apply* the principle of thanking God for all things. David's words, "I will bless the Lord at *all* times . . ." (Ps. 34:1, KJV, italics mine) have become a daily prayer with me. I've thanked God for everything from poor health to radiant health, deplorable setbacks to measurable progress, financial wipe-outs to surprising successes, family feuds to marital joy, frustrating children to delightful children (not to mention a whole batch of other things).

But I had not thanked God for my irregular person! So, a bit gingerly, after Marilyn's whispered comment, I breathed, "Dear Lord, thank you for my irregular person."

You probably won't be surprised to know that nothing, absolutely nothing, happened to my irregular person, but *something* began to change in me. I can only describe the feeling as delicious. *Forgiveness* brought a sweet relief, but *thankfulness* was as delicious as my brownie pie served with real whipped cream and chopped walnuts. To get to the place when you can thank God for your irregular person is, indeed, a wonderful experience!

Those who have your forgiveness up to date and have felt the healing that thankfulness to God brings are probably shouting the old line, "Preach it, lady, I'll turn the pages!" You have seen firsthand the enormous value of Ephesians 5:20 and have identified with every line you've just read.

But there are others reading this right now who play ball in a different league. To be told that Joyce said, "Thank you, Lord" for her irregular person and to read that she described it as a delicious experience is about as comforting as backing into a running buzz saw.

If you are *married* to your irregular person however, you can't put time and distance between you and your mate. You can't escape the poison darts, and your whole existence is filled with daily verbal and nonverbal abuse. You're saying, "Thank God for this mate? No way, José!"

When I have given seminars on irregular people, and when we filmed the *His Stubborn Love* film series, I knew that one of the major drawbacks would be time limitations. All the bases can't be covered in one sixty-minute session or on one film, but we really felt led of the Lord to speak to this issue. Hopefully now, in this book, I can pick up, expand and offer some choices of hope to you who are like the woman in the following letter. She wrote:

Dear Joyce,
I've read several of your books and always found them helpful. But today I listened to your tape, "Your Irregular Person" (Published by Word, 1981), and it really hit home. It was a real blessing as far as it went. But what do you do when your irregular person is your husband?"

Her letter described her life as "nearing unbearable." She tells me that both she and her husband became Christians four years ago, so she says "leaving isn't the answer," but then she describes her life by saying,

Every day is filled to overflowing with pain and disappointment . . . he seldom speaks to me and he hasn't kissed me since last Christmas. . . . I pray each day about it. . . . I believe God answers prayers, but I have had no relief these past ten years, and I'm about to go "out for the count."

As the film on "Irregular People" is being shown all over the world, I am beginning to get an enormous response from viewers. A high percentage of the mail is about an irregular person in someone's life. Many are from women who, like the woman in the letter, are married to their irregular person and are about to go "out for the count."

In searching for wisdom and hopeful solutions for those of you who are married to your irregular person, I was astounded one day by God's leading.

After a short leave of absence, I resumed teaching my Bible study class at Betty Manning's home here in the desert. I was praying about what I should be teaching, and the Lord clearly told me to do a series on women in the Bible. So, I did.

The first session was on Eve. Then, I thought I'd do
Bathsheba. However, you can't teach a lesson on
Bathsheba without talking about David, so I routinely decided to backtrack and reread David's history as a back-
ground for his encounter with Bathsheba. It was in that bit
of homework that I rediscovered a woman I already knew
about—Abigail. But as I read the account in 1 Samuel I
realized, with a slight shock, that Abigail was a woman who
was married to her irregular person! Remember her story?

Abigail was described as being a woman of both beauty
and brains. She was married to a wealthy farmer named
Nabal, who raised huge herds of sheep and goats. Listen to
the words of 1 Samuel, Chapter 25, as it describes Nabal as
being "uncouth, churlish, stubborn and ill-mannered"
(TLB). Even the King James description adds "evil in his
doings." We are not told why Abigail married him in the
first place, or why she stayed with such a lout in the second
place—only that she *did* stay married to him. The only
other thing we are told about Nabal is that he was from the
house of Caleb. All we really know is that, in addition to his
rotten personality, Nabal was probably not a man of God.

Now, the action begins. David, the warrior courtier of
King Saul's court, sends a message to Nabal. He tells him
that he knows Nabal and his men are holding their annual
sheep-shearing festival. He explains that his own army of
soldiers have never stolen from Nabal, but in fact they
have protected Nabal's men and flocks. David ends his
message by asking if Nabal would share some of the food
from their happy holiday with him and his battle-tired men.

Nabal reacts with his typical churlish charm. "Who does
this David think he is? What makes him think I am going to
give him anything?" We can almost hear the snarling ar-
rogance in Nabal's words.

Needless to say, David is not thrilled with Nabal's words
or attitude, and he does not take kindly to the refusal. So, a
furious David and four hundred of his angriest men strap

on their swords and take off over the hills to slaughter Nabal and his men, women, children, and flocks.

Meanwhile, back at the ranch, one of Nabal's hired hands tells Abigail about David's message and Nabal's insulting answer. The servant aptly sums up things by saying to Abigail, "You'd better think fast, for there is going to be trouble for our master and his entire family—he's such a stubborn lout that no one can even talk to him!" (1 Sam. 25:17, TLB).

Abigail, who is known for her beauty *and* brains, takes on an enormous organizational task. She, *without* her husband's knowledge, packs up

> 200 loaves of bread
> 2 barrels of wine
> 5 dressed sheep
> 2 bushels of roasted grain
> and for dessert, she gives
> 100 raisin cakes and
> 200 fig cakes
> (and I think a sit-down dinner
> for eight has its complications!)

Miraculously, Abigail prepares and sends an entire banquet. And then, still without Nabal's knowledge, she rides out to meet with David. (Add, to her beauty and brains, bravery.)

Abigail, when she meets David, bows humbly before him and turns into the first woman with a doctorate in psychology. She speaks and reasons with David, and her words are skillfully and logically spoken. Abigail admits her husband is a fool, as the name Nabal means. She presents David with the food. Then, verbally, she gives David a different perspective of his own attitudes and the possible repercussions of his actions.

David accepts her gifts, weighs what he's been told, and buys her compelling arguments, telling her to return home and assuring her he will not kill Nabal.

Abigail goes back home, presumably to tell Nabal what she has done, but finds him roaring drunk. She has a keenly developed sense of timing, so she decides to wait until morning when he is sober.

The next day, after Abigail tells Nabal how close he came to being annihilated, and that she has given David and his men a banquet, the Bible tells us that Nabal had a stroke and was paralyzed for about ten days. Then he died, as the Scriptures say, for the "Lord killed him" (v. 38, TLB).

What a smashing ending! But it wasn't really the ending. Verses 39–41 reveal, "Then [after Nabal's death] David wasted no time in sending messengers to Abigail to ask her to become his wife. . . . So she became his wife."

This story is only one chapter long, but it is packed with sheer theatrical drama, and its message about being married to an irregular person is crystal clear.

Here are the lessons of Abigail's survival.

1. She used her head—she did not check her brains into a locker for safekeeping. She was no "dumb blonde"; rather, she combined her beauty with intelligent thinking, and it served her well.

2. She was loyal to her irregular husband. She accepted him as he was (a fool, uncouth, churlish, stubborn, and an ill-mannered man) and did not expect him to change.

3. When Nabal's life was in danger she took *extensive* action to save him. She did what was right. She defended him. It's a wonder she didn't pay homage to David, give him the food, and then say, "Nabal is the third guy on the left out there—get him!"

4. Abigail had learned what an important role in life a sense of timing makes. She knew when to speak and when to keep silent. When she did speak, it was with logical yet

gracious wisdom. I could sure take lessons from this lady, especially in the area of her verbal expertise and her balanced sense of timing.

Abigail's plan of survival should speak to all of us, whether we are married to our irregular person or not. This chapter of Samuel does not tell us anything about the hell a person can endure if they are married to their irregular person, but it does tell us everything about Abigail's inner strengths and her healthy emotional and spiritual survival in such a marriage.

The very week I shared Abigail with my Bible-study class, I received the following letter from a present-day Abigail.

Dear Joyce:

I had waited almost a year, praying that you would be at Jesus Northwest in Vancouver my first time there, knowing my life would change because of the message God would have for me through you.

Do you remember sitting at the table in the bookstore, the time growing short till you would have to go? I told you where I was from, and also that I was married to a Mike, my Mike being the "irregular person" in my life. You looked at me with so much compassion and said, "Oh, honey, that's the hardest kind."

Embarrassed, through my tears, I told you of my desire to serve the Lord, like you, through writing and speaking, but 1 Corinthians 7:13 told me I must stay with my unsaved husband. You urged me to pray, believing God would open the doors when His time was right.

That was the day I gave in, accepted my husband unconditionally, gave his drinking problem and our distressed marriage over to God. That day, July 11, I became free, released from anxiety, willing and satisfied to just wait for God to open that door.

September 1 brought a women's Bible study for me to teach, using Charles Allen's book, *God's Psychiatry*. Soon after that, I entered night school, taking English composition. Doors were opening!

On October 3, Ann Kiemel had lunch at my home, and I shared my desires with her. She told me to pray and God would open the door if it was right for me. I informed her that Joyce Landorf had already told me that. . . . Then she asked me if I was prepared for God to prune me, mold me, put me through hardships and trials in order to have something to write about. Hmmmm. Was I?

Eight days later, on October 11, my husband, only thirty-one years of age, died suddenly from a heart attack. This was three months from the day I talked to you.

Joyce, I believe God began to prepare me for my husband's death last July 11 by showing me how to accept my irregular person with the same kind of love that Jesus had for him and for me. He continued to prepare me by leading me into Isaiah 54 just prior to Mike's death, and He filled my life with His loving people.

I do not live in the sorrows of my widowhood, for my Creator is my husband. He is truly supplying all my needs. I've been invited to take speaker's training for Christian Women's Club. Wow!! I got an "A" on my finals in writing class. Wow, again!! Joyce, God just never takes anything from us but what he gives us something in return!

I do not know what special, exciting plan He has for me, but I need to tell you, Joyce, thank you for being there when I needed you and for being the special woman of God that you are. Through you God has released me from myself, taught me how to serve, to seek, to love, to know peace, and to WAIT!

I plan to be at Jesus Northwest again this year, and will be praying for you and hope to see you there.

God be with you . . . thank you.

Now, that's a letter written by an Abigail-type survivor! It would be entirely too simplistic to say that, because God removed Nabal from Abigail's life and Dick from my young friend's life, we can count on the Lord to do the same for us. Absolutely not. We must *never* limit God to Plan A, B, or C. I'm not about to promise that if you obey the Lord, accept your husband as he is, and keep a right standing with God, He will remove your husband and in ten days you'll marry the future king of Israel!

Nor am I saying that God will honor your obedience and that your irregular and/or unsaved husband or wife will miraculously come to know the Lord, thus solving all your problems.

I *do* have a few precious letters that tell me God indeed rescued and changed their irregular person. Such a letter was this one from a woman who wrote:

> My father would have to be the irregular person in my life. He was an alcoholic, and put our family through a living hell while we were growing up.
>
> Often I grew impatient, and wondered why God did not hear our cries and cure him.
>
> I even wondered why God just wouldn't allow something to happen to my father. That's how desperate I felt.
>
> But it's all over now, and I can see God's plan for my father so perfectly. You see, I did not know then that God also loved my dad, sinner that he was, and did not want him to be damned forever.
>
> After my dear mother died of M.S. at the age of fifty-four, and all of us children were gone from home, my father drank himself into a state of severe illness and had to be hospitalized. And there, finally, a pastor was able to reach him and bring him into God's kingdom.
>
> A year after that God allowed an automobile accident to take my father's life—on Ash Wednesday as he was coming home from a church service where he had taken part in the Lord's Supper. My irregular person is now in heaven— praise the Lord!

In this case God intervened—and we must not close the door to God's mysterious, but miraculous workings. However, I want you to read these next few words very slowly:

*God **may** change your irregular mother, father, or relative. The Holy Spirit **may** convict and convince your husband or wife, and they **may** come to a saving knowledge of Christ.* I've used the word *may* three times because, again, I do not want to limit our all-powerful God or put Him in a box. God will work this out in your life as He chooses to, and in His time, as He did with this alcoholic father. But do not be misled or deceived—*God **may not** choose to work in the way you expect.*

Also, I have noticed that some people, if they are married to an *unsaved* irregular person, seem to think that all he or she needs is to know the Lord. Now, there is nothing more true than that. All *anyone* needs in his or her life is the Lord. And, if your irregular husband or wife comes to know Jesus, he or she *will* be changed . . . or will they? I'm afraid there is another side of the coin to consider.

I have a large stack of letters from women who are married to their irregular person. There are perhaps one hundred fifty or so. Of those letters, fifty-five are from women whose irregular husband (are you ready for this?) is a pastor, minister, or is involved in full-time Christian work!

Coming to Christ does not give a guarantee that irregular people will have their crippling childhood, inborn genetic temperament, or mental capabilities all suddenly erased or changed. True, our irregular people are new creatures in Christ when they come to Him. But if they are not obedient to the Lord, if they walk after the flesh, and flaunt, as it were, their standing with God, old habits and attitudes will hang on. They will experience little of God's transforming power in their lives.

How I wish that *all* of us would *always* allow God to do His needed work in our lives, but sometimes we choose less than His best.

My own irregular person has known and loved the Lord for many years, so the easy answer of "he just needs to know the Lord" is simply not the solution. Irregular people are not always *capable* of changing lifelong personality patterns. They are like a blind person, as I've stated before, who cannot *make* himself see.

So what's the answer here? I think Abigail understood it best. I believe she forgave herself and God for their marriage: she harbored no self-pity; and, at some time, she must have thanked God for Nabal. He was her husband, for better or for worse, and when she saw he probably would never change, *she* changed. *She* took up the enormous, challenging burden, and *she* did what God required of her.

It seems to me that we cannot *count on* anything changing our irregular person (*though I know God can and does—sometimes, if he or she is open to it*). I'm only saying we must not live minute by minute, counting on the illusive dream and the longed-for hope that this will be the day. God's timing rarely comes across as logical to us.

As I read the Abigail story over again today, I found myself caring more about how Abigail survived than I did about whether Nabal would wondrously turn into a great and glorious husband. So it is with any of you who are married to your irregular person. I pray your husband or wife allows God to change him or her, but what I really care the most about is your hope in Christ, your ability to live in joy and peace, and your godly survival.

Please don't think I believe your husband (or my own irregular person) can *never* be changed by God. I know about the power of Jesus, and the God I love and serve is *more* than capable of changing the seemingly impossible person. It's just that I do not want you to fall into the same trap I did. Remember the words of Dr. Dobson's letter, which I received eight years ago? He wrote, "I think you are still hoping your irregular person will miraculously become what he has never been . . ." I know it does hurt less if we do not spend every waking hour expecting and hoping our irregular person will change.

It is my prayer, as you read these pages, that we will share a common hope and even that, in experiencing this difficult relationship, you and I will both change. I pray also that you and I will reflect the joy and strength of the Lord, and that we will live lives pleasing to the Lord—giving thanks for everything.

I read an anonymous piece the other day that said:

We cannot control the length of our life
But we can control its width and depth.
We cannot control the contour of our face
But we can control its expressions.
We cannot control someone else's opportunities
But we can grasp our own.
We cannot control another person's annoying faults
But we can see that we do not develop or harbor provoking practices.
We cannot control someone else's relationship to God
But we can be sure about our own salvation.

Actually, bringing our own personal forgiveness up to date and choosing to thank God for our irregular persons is really positive proof that we are well on the road to inner healing. We are beginning to be survivors!

CHAPTER SEVEN

THE CONFERENCE IN ARLINGTON, Texas, had already begun. I was scheduled to speak that evening, but my flight arrangements had put me into town early. I slipped into the auditorium as the afternoon session was in progress.

Only later did I realize the magnitude of how very special God had been to me that day.

The speaker was an Asbury Seminary professor named Dr. Robert Mulholland, and his topic was suffering. He could not have known my specific circumstances, yet in his talk it was as if he addressed himself to each painful issue in my struggle with suffering. There were several hundred people present, but I felt the spoken words were just for me.

I was at a fragile point in coping with some very primary needs. Basically, I was trying to maintain some semblance of physical, spiritual, and emotional equilibrium. It was a very narrow balance beam. Cautiously I was trying to find a way to keep myself stabilized between the crushing suffering of physical pain and the annihilating suffering of emotional pain as I tried to cope with my irregular person.

The first part of Dr. Mulholland's lecture eased my mind into a substantial breakthrough in understanding what I think is a theological truth: suffering is *definitely* a part of the Christian's life. It is a part we *hope* will be utterly minimized or, as my positive-thinking friends say, it will

126

turn quickly into joyous experiences, but it *is* a part of living nevertheless! And often suffering does not grind slowly to a halt, but rather merely grinds on.

The scriptures that the speaker chose left little doubt that suffering is certainly allowed by God, and that many times it is a *necessary* and *vital* part of God's plan. The verses in Deuteronomy 32:39 and Hosea 6:1 do not reveal a vindictive God, a God who acts on malicious impulses or goes on random rampages to punish us, but rather a just and completely righteous God. I began to see the character and the formidable sovereignty of God as I'd never seen it before.

Suffering, as Dr. Mulholland described it, has been a part of God's plan not only for mankind, but for his own Son Jesus as well. The book of Hebrews reveals, "But we do see Jesus—who for awhile was a little lower than the angels—crowned now by God with glory and honor because he suffered death for us. Yes, because of *God's great kindness*, Jesus tasted death for everyone in all the world. And it was right and proper that God, who made everything for his own glory, should allow Jesus to suffer, for in doing this he was bringing vast multitudes of God's people to heaven; for his *suffering* made Jesus a perfect leader, one fit to bring them into their salvation" (Heb. 2:9–10, TLB, italics mine).

As Dr. Mulholland continued, I sat there stunned with the reality that if out of "God's great kindness" Jesus suffered even unto death—who was I to resent physical or emotional pain? Had I not said a thousand times, in a thousand rededication-commitment-renewal services, "Lord use me, I don't care what the price—just use me?"

When the price turned out to be several forms of expensive suffering, I had rejected the whole ball of wax. *Why would a LOVING God do this to me?* I had shouted to myself. Then, in this conference, the scripture in Hebrews came undeniably clear. Actually, suffering is one of the most effective ways God has to make His people—even His own son—*usable*. The scriptures in Hebrews just clearly said that suffering was the price of making Jesus a perfect leader! How easy it is to ignore the doctrine of suffering in the Bible and to slip on the blinders of denial about the beautiful purposes of suffering.

You well may be asking, at this moment, why all this emphasis on suffering? What has God's allowing suffering got to do with surviving endless rounds of stress and conflict between myself and my irregular person?

Only this. If you are to be a survivor, you'll need a firm understanding of suffering. If you are to grow spiritually and turn the irregular relationship into a fruitful, productive experience, you'll need to grasp the significance of our sovereign God's attitudes about suffering.

Over the years I've been examining what the Word says about suffering, and as I listened to Professor Mulholland that day I remembered Romans 8. That's where Paul speaks directly to my sufferings. He writes about what it means to be children of God, and he says, "If we are his children we share his treasures, and all that Christ claims as his will belong to all of us as well! Yes, if we share in his sufferings we shall certainly share in his glory" (Rom. 8:17, Phillips).

I do believe, however, the hardest and biggest word in the last line of verse 17 is *if*. "*If* we share." One translation puts it this way: "*presuming* that we suffer" (MLB). It seems to me that during most of my Christian processing experience I have lightly skipped the "if" in this scripture and jumped with both feet into the next verse.

"For I reckon that the sufferings of this present time are not worthy to be compared with the glory which shall be revealed in us" (Rom. 8:18, KJV). Here's where my timing differs with God's. I can readily accept an instant or two of suffering and years of glory, but I'm well convinced that's not what God had in mind when He wrote through Paul's pen.

I suppose, as I reflect again on Dr. Mulholland's presentation that day in Texas, what really touched my heart the most was what he called his "exercises of healing." First, the professor suggested, we focus in on the aspect (or a personal relationship) of our life that we *know* needs healing. Next, Dr. Mulholland suggested, we thank God for this whole thing—whatever or whoever it is.

As I've already related, this second exercise was a previously crossed bridge for me; I had already thanked God for my irregular person. (The speaker's words brought a credible confirmation to my heart and told me I'd done the right thing.) However, the next suggestion given to us that day, as part of the exercises for healing, was very new to me. Dr. Mulholland talked about relinquishing ourselves in the need for healing, turning it over to the Lord, and giving God (of all things!) the *permission* to do whatever He needed to do *through* this situation, circumstance, or relationship.

For a moment I puzzled over "giving God permission." Did God need my permission—or was that what the speaker meant? About then Dr. Mulholland tied together our giving God permission with his final point: yielding ourselves to the Lord in all of this. My notes tell me that his exact words were, "Allow the Lord to peel away the dragon skins like He did to Eustace in C. S. Lewis's *The Chronicles of Narnia.*"

The name Eustace rang an old familiar bell in my head, but I'd forgotten the details. Did you ever read aloud to your children the fantasy stories of C. S. Lewis that tell about the adventures of Peter, Susan, Edmund, and Lucy in the land of Narnia? I have. And even if I reach my eighties, I will still find these marvelously written books timeless in their creative appeal and their outpouring of practical applications of Christianity. The genius of C. S. Lewis continues to be a thing of beauty to me, although I must admit his formidable intellectual abilities sometimes leave me shaking my head, wondering, "Now, what did he say?" But, back to Eustace. I borrowed a friend's book and reread the story.

The first lines of Book 3 in the series, entitled *Voyage of the Dawn Treader*, read, "There was a boy called Eustace Clarence Scrubb, and he almost deserved it. His parents called him Eustace Clarence and his school masters called him Scrubb. I can't tell how his friends spoke of him for he had none."[1]

Eustace, as Lewis describes him, is a rather horrible boy who, while on an adventure on a very strange island, turns into a fire-breathing dragon. Then Eustace meets a great, golden-maned lion. (In all of the Narnia stories, the lion is named Aslan, and is always symbolic of the spirit and character of God.) When Eustace—now turned into a dragon—meets this majestic lion, he is *compelled* to follow him. The lion leads the dragon a long way over the meadows and valleys. Eventually they wind up in the mountains at a place with a large, bubbling, crystal-clear pool in the middle of a beautiful garden.

The lion communicates (somehow without words) that the dragon should bathe in the waters. Eustace thinks this is a fine idea, and the bubbling waters look very healing and soothing. But, the lion tells him that he must first undress.

Obediently (this is totally out of character for him), Eustace begins to peel off his dragon skin. He removes the skin and takes a few steps down into the water, only to find there is another layer of dragon skin still on him! Twice more he peels off the ugly outer skin only to have it replace itself.

Finally, the lion tells Eustace that he will have to let him undress him. The dragon agrees that this is the only way, so he lays down on his back and the skinning begins.

The lion, using his huge, sharp claws, begins pulling off the heavy, rough, dragon skin, and it hurts worse than *anything* Eustace has ever felt before. But finally all the layers of skin are really off, and they are off to stay.

The lion throws the newly peeled dragon into the water and, though he smarts a little at first, the dragon soon finds he is pain-free for the first time. Then, to his great surprise, Eustace finds himself turned back, once more, into his original shape. He has been transformed from an ugly, fire-breathing dragon to a boy—and a *changed* boy at that. He heads back down the mountain to find the other children and to show and tell them about his extraordinary encounter with the lion. He begins to lose his horrid-boy traits and, as C. S. Lewis comments, "The cure had begun."

Professor Mulholland made the astute observation that lying down, yielding ourselves to the Lord, and giving God permission to do whatever "peeling" was needed means that basically we have to understand *that the process might hurt*. (Aha! A vital point in the doctrine of suffering, I believe.)

In that special moment, as I sat among the listeners in that auditorium, I laid my aching head and my battered emotions down by the bubbling water's edge and said to the Lord, "Go ahead. Peel off the layers of my painful conflict, and do it now. I would be changed, like Eustace—from dragon to person—and made whole." And another inner healing took place.

Not too long after that conference, Psalm 4:3–5 helped my understanding of how yielding really works in a practical way. (You'll notice that I've set the lines apart for clarity and emphasis.)

Mark this well:
The Lord has set apart the redeemed for himself. Therefore he will listen to me and answer when I call to him.
[Now, notice all the verbs—the "to do" words]
Stand before the Lord in awe, and
do not sin against him.

Lie quietly upon your bed in silent meditation.
Put your trust in the Lord, and
Offer him pleasing sacrifices

(Ps. 4:3–5, TLB, italics mine).

Here is the essence of these scriptures: When we really yield ourselves to the Lord, we respectfully *stand* before Him *without* sinning; we *lie* quietly to "be still and know"; we *put* our trust and confidence into no one but the Lord; and we *offer* our lives (body and soul) to Him as a living sacrifice. The suffering may hurt, and we may never like the peeling process but, oh, being healed and attaining a right standing with God is worth it all. The process hurts and heals almost in one encounter. And the release that comes with yielding defies description!

Giving God permission to do what He must, and yielding ourselves to Him as part of the healing process, means we are enabled to see our irregular person from a new and incredibly different perspective.

My irregular person remains the same as always. But *I've* changed. And, wonder of wonders, as I

• implement the forgiveness principles,
• thank God for my person,
• give permission to God to use this situation, and
• yield myself to surrender to the Lord,

each encounter, phone call, letter, or visit with my irregular person becomes *less* devastating than the one before. I'm surviving—more than that, I'm coping.

Last, but not least, comes the knowledge that this healing and coping process can be a peaceful one. It can also be a restorative process in my life, if I firmly understand God's concept of suffering and know the exact parameters of my spiritual beliefs.

My daughter-in-love, Teresa, was on the phone with me a while back, and we were talking about my chronic jaw and head problems with Temporomandibular Joint Stress

Dysfunction, or T.M.J., the painful syndrome which has given me so much distress over a number of years. At one point in our conversation, she said something about "I *believe* the Lord is going to do such-and-such about this horrible pain. . . ." I can't recall what it was that she said she believed, because at that moment I was nearly deafened by my own shouting inner question: "What *exactly* do *you* believe, Joyce?" What is my rock-bottom belief about my jaw pain? About my suffering? About the continual darts my irregular person hurls at me? What is it that I really *believe* with my whole heart?

I realized that, in regard to my irregular person, I would truly love to believe that God is going to intervene and change him. In fact, I've had this fantasy that my irregular person phones me and the conversation goes like this:

"Hello, Joyce. I'd like to talk to you about a serious thing I have on my heart."

"Yes, of course. Go ahead."

"Well, first of all, I want to talk about the past."

"Okay, good. What about the past?"

He pauses and begins so haltingly that I know what he is about to say is *very* difficult for him to verbalize.

"It's just that," he continues, "I've been thinking and going over things in our past; and it seems to me there are some events I should have never let happen and some words that I *should* have spoken.

"I've been insensitive to you and (here he names others in the family) and to the needs of your lives. I want to tell you that I know I've hurt the family and you by my responses or my lack of responses."

Then he cites other painful examples and quietly says he was to blame. Now, for the first time in our relationship, he shoulders the responsibility for his words and actions, and simply stuns me by ending with, "I'm sorry those things happened. I don't even know the whys of it all—only that I'm asking your forgiveness. I don't want to die before I clear this up. This is some unfinished business in my life, and I'm truly sorry."

Before I can respond, he adds, "And one more thing, Joyce. I want you to know I love you. I always have, but I just couldn't say it outright, and my actions never bore out that love. I'm sorry."

I have fantasized for some time the warm healing which would pour over my cold and heavily embattled soul. I tearfully interrupt him to affirm my love for him. I tell him over and over how everything is all right now. How I have *already* forgiven him, how I have *already* accepted him. Then I ask for his forgiveness as well. I tell him I love him, that I'm not angry anymore, and that I *believed* someday things would be right between us.

End of fantasy.

Why? Because I don't really *believe* this conversation will take place. I wish it would, but wishing and believing are two roads which go in opposite directions.

Let me quickly reassure you that I'm not ruling out any of the scriptures which tell us that "nothing is impossible with God" (Matt. 19:26, Mark 10:27, Luke 1:37, and 18:27, to name a few). It's just that I cannot face every morning *believing* that this will be the day I'll hear the words I so long to hear. This fantasy of mine very well may *never* happen, and the sooner I understand that and adjust to it, the quicker the healing process and the smoother the coping will be.

My question is: What, then, do I really *believe* about my irregular person?

Here it is. No great theological concept, no big intellectual philosophy, and no intricately delicate solution. Just this: *I believe God knows what He is doing.*

You and I may never, in all of God's green earth, understand the bone-bare reasons for the unfairness, the injustice, and the hideous pain of life in our sometimes pit-level existence. But we can run—no, fly with wings of eagles—if the bottom line of our spiritual beliefs is that we *believe God knows what He is doing.*

The day this belief really etched itself indelibly into my mind was September 19, 1980. I had set aside the first weeks of September, with no speaking engagements, because our daughter, Laurie, was to have her first baby. I was really looking forward to it.

Teresa, our daughter-in-love, had given birth to her second child, Ricky, in July of that same year. I was there at the hospital but, because she had a C-section delivery, I could not see the birth or be with her. The girls and their doctor (my favorite gynecologist), Dr. Bhatt, had invited me to both births, and since I'd missed Teresa's delivery I was really counting on being with Laurie.

However, by the sixteenth of September Laurie was still very pregnant. I had to speak in Cedar Rapids and Des Moines, Iowa, on the eighteenth and nineteenth. I called Laurie and told her that if she wanted me to cancel out Iowa I would. Evidently she had given it considerable thought, because instantly and beautifully she responded, "Mom, go. They need you in Des Moines. Just go. The Lord will take care of the situation here." Reluctantly I agreed, and said, "Okay. But this is Wednesday. I'll be home Saturday. Cross your legs and don't *do* anything!"

I left California, confident in the belief that God would honor Laurie's obedient attitude. I *believed* the Lord would give her the baby on Saturday—after I got home.

When I got to Des Moines, Lonna Field drove me to Cedar Rapids. I spoke, did TV and radio interviews, and got back to my hotel in Des Moines very late the night of the eighteenth. Around midnight my phone rang. It was my son-in-love, Terry, and he said, "We have a little boy . . . his name is James Andrew."

Since Terry had called me several times in the previous weeks and had jokingly exclaimed, with great excitement in his voice, "We *don't* have a baby yet!" I thought this was another display of Terry's sense of humor. So I said, right off the bat, "Oh, no you don't! You're not serious! You're just kidding me! You wouldn't dare have that baby while I'm gone!" But softly Terry assured me that it was true.

I still didn't believe him, so I asked to speak to Laurie. Her first words were, "Mom, we have a sweet little boy."

The feelings which were beginning to rise in me felt more like white-hot wrath than mild frustration. I could feel myself getting very angry, especially at the Lord. I had *believed* He would let me be a part of Laurie's birthing experience. I had *believed* that the Lord would allow me not only to be in the alternate birthing room at the hospital with Laurie, but also to be the one who would support her back as she delivered. Yet none of what I had *believed* had happened.

Laurie sensed that the reason I wasn't responding to her on the phone was that I was crying. Now we were both crying.

"Mom, Mom," I finally heard her say. "Listen, the Lord did a really neat thing today." Then Laurie went on to explain that the nurse who came on duty to take care of her in the early stages of her labor was wearing my brand of perfume. "You smell like my Mom," Laurie had blurted out. Then Laurie had explained to the woman that *I* couldn't be with her, so she had prayed that her mother's spirit would be there . . . and then the nurse had come in wearing my perfume. They had begun to talk, and Laurie had found out that Monica was a Christian.

In the conversation to follow, Monica asked Laurie why her mother wasn't there. Did she live in Des Moines or what? So Laurie told her I was speaking in Iowa, and finally Monica asked, "Who is your mother? What's her name?"

Laurie said on the phone, "Mom, we almost lost a good nurse there!" It turned out that Monica had read my books and had always wanted to thank me in person. Then she had come on duty only to discover her patient was Joyce

Landorf's daughter. We will always be grateful for the numerous kindnesses Monica, Mary Jean, and Dr. Bhatt gave to our Laurie that day.

However, when I hung up the phone, in Iowa, I was still angry. Laurie had assured me, over and over again, that everything was fine and that Saturday would come soon enough, yet the angry feelings kept gnawing at me. I cried for a couple of hours, and finally crept into bed—a physical and emotional basket case.

I was dressed and ready to go to the civic auditorium by eight o'clock on the morning of September nineteenth, but never was I more belligerent or reluctant to speak!

I felt betrayed. I'd trusted God. I'd *believed* that God would let me have the joy of seeing my two grandbabies being born. But now both babies were here, and I'd missed both births.

Just before I left the hotel, I remembered Teresa's phone call, my question of what do I believe, and suddenly the truth of my "belief" statement hit me. *I really do believe God knows what He is doing.*

Just after I arrived at the civic center, I met with Joey Paul, Bob Wolgemuth, and Chris Hayward—from Word Publishing. They were there to observe the seminars and to give a final decision on doing the *His Stubborn Love* film series. I remember telling them about missing James' birth, how angry I was, and that all I had to hang on to was that I *believed* God knew what He was doing. Bob prayed a marvelous prayer for all of us, and I went out on stage with a fresh commitment to the Lord.

Since I have always leveled with audiences, I said, "I don't want to be here in Des Moines today. I want to be in California with my daughter, Laurie. She gave birth to her first baby yesterday while I was in Cedar Rapids, and I missed the whole thing. But now I *am* here, and she and little James are there. And I'll admit that, while I don't understand it or like it one bit, I *believe* God knows what

He is doing. And there is someone sitting out there who God has here today, who needs to hear this seminar, and He will minister to that person. Maybe it will be just one woman, but I *know* I'm here for somebody today, and God's going to make this a very special time."

Of the thousand-plus women who attended that day, it seemed that at least four hundred fifty women told me with all certainty, during the first coffee break, "*I'm the woman*." After that, it happened all day—hundreds of women, *knowing* that God had met their needs, assured me that my trip was not in vain or even ill-timed. It was beautiful!

After the fourth seminar session ended late in the afternoon, I signed books for over an hour. At one point, I glanced down the long line of women waiting for me and one woman caught my attention. Because of the gray color of her skin I thought, *cancer.*

When she finally reached me, she did not give me a book to sign. She simply asked, "Will you do me a favor?" I said yes, and asked her what. Then, very deliberately, she said, "When you go home, I want you to thank Laurie and Terry for letting you come to Des Moines. I am the woman that God wanted you to minister to . . . I'm the one He wanted to reach. Please thank them for me."

With a remarkably steady voice she briefly told me that two years ago she had discovered she had cancer, and that she had been doing just fine. But, for the last couple of months, everything had been going wrong. She talked of pain and the severe depression that comes with it, and of her inability and unwillingness to move into acceptance. Her next words were, "Then you came out on that stage this morning and said that you believed God knew what He was doing—even without our *understanding* it, without our *seeing* Him work, and without our *feeling* His presence. By this afternoon, I'd gone from depression to acceptance, and I'm going home to be the woman, the wife, and the mother to my children that God wants me to be, and for as long as I have time."

The grayness never left her face as she talked with me, the cancer did not lift off her fragile body, nor do I know the state of her well-being right now. But *I believe God knows what He is doing*—even in my being in Iowa instead of California. God had everything planned in the right way, and that brief conversation was the proof of God's great, caring heart.

What do I believe? I know what I *can't* believe. Especially when it comes to my irregular person. I don't believe my irregular person is going to allow the Lord to change him, so I have to come back to what I *do* believe. Actually, I come back time and time again to cling to the belief that *God knows* what He is doing. This keeps a song alive in my heart, and this keeps a potentially dangerous attitude from growing in the soil of bitterness.

There is one more positive step towards the coping and healing of our spirits in regard to irregular people and that is a prayer. It's a prayer that we must constantly breathe, check out, and keep in the frontal lobes of our brains. It goes something like this:

> Lord, don't let me fall into the trap of being an irregular person to anyone in my family. Especially in regard to my relationship with my children. Help me to identify and deal with any irregular tendencies in myself, for I do not want to risk creating and raising children who grow into crippled adults, unable to express empathy or relate to others. Keep the desire strong to be regular, to verbalize affirmation, to freely apologize, to quickly restore harmony, to be willing to accept and overlook the faults in others. Keep me teachable and willing to change the faults in me.
>
> I don't want to be handicapped, limited, or irregular to anyone else in the whole world. Keep my heart tender to your Holy Spirit, Lord, and use the lessons of pain I've

learned from my irregular person to stretch my mind and soul into the pattern *you* desire.

And Lord, one more thing, I *do* believe you know what you are doing—and I trust you with my whole heart.

CHAPTER EIGHT

WHEN I BEGAN WRITING THIS BOOK almost a year ago, I did not have any idea it would take this long to complete. Nor did I envision an eighth chapter.

I felt that in seven chapters I could concentrate sufficiently on most of the lessons the Lord has been teaching me, over the past years, about irregular people. I would share your letters and conversations, because your insights and personal examples have provided documentation and a credible map for the unexplored territory of irregular relationships. I knew how I could detail the Lord's guidance, as He helped me to expose and deal with the greatest emotional pain of my life. But, mostly I would make this a positive book of hope (not only to you, but to myself), to remind us how our God continually and compassionately gives us the ability to joyfully survive in spite of these irregular relationships.

I did not want to include (or add to what I've already written of and shared in the film series) anything of the intensity of my struggles with physical pain. In my own mind, they were two completely different issues.

What I failed to consider, until just recently, was how very much my chronic bouts with jaw and head pain have altered my life. This daily pain has immeasurably warped my attitudes, responses, and behavior towards others. And it has vastly changed ("destroyed" is a better word) my abilities to think and write.

All during this sporadic year of writing, I have fervently tried to separate the emotional pain caused by my irregular person from the daily physical pain I am experiencing. It has not worked well at all, for *both* kinds of pain are inexplicably bound together within me.

To write about one kind of pain and not the other is to miss the mark, if—emotionally and physically—we are to understand, cope, and experience any kind of healing.

So I find myself at the eighth chapter, filled with the same familiar reluctance that I wrote about in my letter to you at the beginning. But I will listen to the gentle stirrings in my own heart, and pray God does for you what He has done for me (and others) so that we may be *whole*, not fragmented, people of God.

This past year has been both the best and the worst time of my life.

The best year because God has poured out His benefits and blessings on our families, our children, and our grandchildren. He has anointed my books, tapes, film series, and personal appearances with an outpouring of His Spirit. I am truly blessed. During this year, thousands of God's people have lovingly and beautifully prayed for me and dearly ministered to my suffering on a touching level that defies description. I continue to wake each morning surprised at God's faithful goodness.

But *the worst year* of my life has also become a reality. Because, in this bountiful harvest-time of my life, and in spite of the many prayers for my physical healing, the Lord has chosen to let my jaw and head pain not only stay with me, but intensify.

C. S. Lewis expressed a theory that God whispers to us in our pleasures, He speaks to us in our consciousness, and He shouts to us in our pain.

I think God *has* to shout to us in pain because the agony

of suffering is so deafening. But, in this past year, I've alternated between hearing the shouting of God and understanding the silence of God. It's all been so puzzling.

Perhaps for you, too, this has been a year of frightening heights and depths. Or, as Charles Dickens once wrote, in *A Tale of Two Cities:*

> It was the best of times, it was the worst of times, it was the age of wisdom, it was the age of foolishness, it was the epoch of belief, it was the epoch of incredulity, it was the season of Light, it was the season of Darkness, it was the spring of hope, it was the winter of despair.

I'm sure, like me, you have had your moments of springtime, filled with hope; and then, in almost an instant, you have been plunged into the wintertime of despair . . . especially when it comes to your rapport with your irregular person.

I hear you clearly. And I can easily slip into your shoes. It also occurs to me that, like me, you feel you've done everything within your power to deal with the emotional pain caused by your irregular person. Perhaps you've *already* done everything this book has suggested, or you are in the process of acting upon all or some of the guidelines set down here. But, in either case, there still is a gut-level pain that insidiously comes and goes, eating whole parts of your life away.

This chapter is just for you.

A few months ago, I was satisfied that I was doing all that could be done in coping and dealing with my irregular person. But, because of this gnawing emotional inner pain and an even greater physical pain being mixed up together, I wondered if maybe I'd overlooked something and had missed some vital lesson from the Lord.

Then, without mentally connecting my emotional pain with my jaw problem, I was referred to a doctor who was a specialist in diagnosing and finding causes for cranial pain.

His reputation preceded him, and it was truly illustrious. His genius lay in the fact that he was generally able to pinpoint problems and get to the *root* causes of pain in the patients sent to him, even when other doctors had tried and failed.

At the end of my first visit, he told me that he was looking for a needle in a haystack in order to find a cause or cure for my pain. The doctor also wanted to know if I'd be willing to undergo a number of intensive questioning sessions which would cover a wide range of subjects. I agreed. (When you have undergone chronic pain for more than one year—I'd had six—you find yourself desperately agreeing to just about anything!) Besides, I'd tried all the conventional methods I'd heard of to correct and alleviate T.M.J. pain—now it was time for the *un*conventional.

For many weeks I drove the almost three hundred miles to be examined, probed, tested, and—mostly—questioned. I was asked about everything having to do with my health, and was quizzed in depth about my personal and public life. We talked over the books I'd already written, and dwelt a long time on this one. No stone was left unturned, and no haystack had ever been more thoroughly searched.

Early in the series of sessions, it became apparent that there was hardly any way I could discuss my physical pain without also touching upon my emotional pain in regard to my irregular person. So, as clinically and as succinctly as I could, I began. And, though this doctor was not a psychiatrist, I spread out the messages that were filling my mind, poured out my long pent-up emotions, and gave detailed descriptions of the now unbearable head pain.

When fall came, and my speaking-schedule dates were packed like sardines on my calendar, I explained to the doctor that I'd be unable to continue our office visits. Without a whole lot of hope or enthusiasm, I asked him if he'd found the needle (or even a small pin) in the haystack of my pain.

He solemnly shook his head yes. The doctor explained that he'd not found any cure for the pain, but that he believed he had found some important connections.

He began talking to me about some unique, God-given strengths I had been given. Strangely enough, these were strengths I had been taught were weaknesses by my irregular person. I said very, very little, but listened closely as an esteemed member of the medical profession laid bare some important concepts about my own self-worth. In short, he gave me a view of myself from another perspective. I will never forget his words for, from that day to this, I am perceiving myself and my strengths in a different way. To have years of preconditioning turned around in the opposite direction was an incredible thing to experience. I built a mental altar of thanksgiving to the Lord for this dedicated man.

The doctor had been quietly talking to me for some time, and I really thought he was about to bring me his conclusions, when abruptly he said, "Now, Joyce, I've got to talk to you about another matter . . . your irregular person." And, before I could react, he added, "Because there is a definite connection between him and your pain."

Then I listened for the better part of an hour as he described some of the major areas in which my irregular person had consistently hurt me over the years. I was stunned as the doctor accurately described my earlier feelings of anger, bitterness, and abandonment. But I was completely surprised when he described in detail the *exact* incident that, like the proverbial straw, had broken the camel's back.

It is not germane to this writing to reveal the details of the moment, or of the doctor's theory. But I knew that the incident which he described (involving my irregular person) corresponded to the exact second in my life when the *physical* pain began. I had never put the two things together.

The doctor explained it was as if my whole body and soul had gone on overload. My physical and emotional resistance had been down, so consequently all the darts shot from my irregular person had found the targets within me. Its effect, the doctor pointed out, had been like a massive coronary, a stroke, or a grand mal epileptic seizure; the inside of me resembled a massive battle ground—terribly wounded and probably scarred forever.

Everything within me had broken down, and the emotional pain had been joined by penetrating physical pain. The doctor was right. I knew he spoke the truth, because God instantly confirmed it in my soul.

The doctor let me sit there for a moment in a numb silence. Then he asked, "May I tell you, now, what I see when I look at you?"

I nodded.

"Well, *outwardly* I see a woman who is coping magnificently with her irregular person. I haven't the faintest idea *how* you have achieved that." (Had I been able to think or talk at that point, I could have given him a quick verbal outline of several of these chapters.)

"Each time we have talked about your irregular person," the doctor related, "there has been no anger in your voice, no trace of bitterness in your spirit. And you have consistently spoken of him in loving terms of forgiveness." He smiled and shook his head. "You are doing beautifully as you cope with your irregular person on a day-to-day basis. You are functioning and in control of the most distressing and stressful relationship in your life . . . and, frankly, I'm amazed!

"However, I am now going to tell you what I see *inside* of you." He took a deep breath, and his words, although spoken gently and softly, filled his office and reverberated in my soul as loudly as if a freight train had roared past us and through the room.

"*Inwardly, I see a completely different story altogether.*

146

I can see you are filled, from the top of your head to the soles of your feet, with massive, unhealed scars. Some of those wounds were made by your irregular person long ago, in your childhood; others, he gave you recently. But they are all unhealed, raw, and hemorrhaging.

"Skillfully you have hidden the existence and the magnitude of these hurts from your family and the world around you, but you know what I've just said is true."

The veracity of his information and perceptive insight left me breathless. I felt vulnerable and totally naked. I remember thinking, as I began to recover my senses, *Now he is going to suggest I go see a psychiatrist.* But, he didn't. Instead, he gently touched my face and said kindly, "Joyce, there isn't a doctor or another human being in the whole world who can heal the vastness of your wounds. *Only the Lord can do it.* And I believe He will."

The doctor talked for another few minutes, using exact, precise examples from my relationship with my irregular person to back up his theory, and I listened in a dazed silence. Once again the Lord confirmed the truth of his words within my heart and mind.

Finally it was time to drive home. I mumbled my good-byes, and vaguely heard the doctor repeat that he believed God would heal the hidden inner hurts of my life. He asked if I would write to him if something changed in regard to my pain. Unable to speak, I nodded my head and found my way out of his office.

I drove for a few miles on the freeway, with the doctor's words and information repeating over and over again in my mind, like a broken record. It was as though both my driving and my thoughts had switched to automatic pilot. I found myself mechanically pulling off the freeway and driving to a large shopping mall, where I parked my car and spent two hours idly walking in and out of one shop after another. I saw nothing. I talked to no one. I heard only the doctor's quiet words.

Finally, I made my way back to the car and the freeway. The huge green-and-white directional sign above my driving lane indicating the "Newport I-55 Tustin" exit brought me back to earth and reality. Immediately the doctor's recorded messages stopped running on the tapes of my mind, and I began this conversation with the greatest of physicians, the Lord Himself.

So clearly, I remember saying, "Lord, for the first time in my life, another human being, a professional medical person, has looked deeply inside of me and seen what no one else here on earth has *ever* seen. The experience has left me shaken and fearful. He has seen and described to me my inner self as even I have never dared to probe or examine. He has, in his own way, pronounced that my wounds are so severe I shall die from them if they are left raw and bleeding. But, perceptive man that he is, he has accurately referred me to You. You, Jesus, are the only physician that can stop the writhing, pounding pain or put an end to my inner dying.

"So, I come before You, Lord, with over forty years of emotional pain and seven years of physical pain, desperate for Your healing touch. My torn, ravaged emotions and my terribly painful memories need You . . . and only You.

"Thank You for the outside of me. Thank You for producing and allowing Your forgiveness to flow through me, so I could cope with my irregular person.

"Thank You for Your divine plan, which placed my irregular person in my life for growing, stretching, and developing.

"Thank You for germinating, through my contacts with my irregular person, the seeds of the fruits of the Spirit in my words and actions.

"Thank You for helping me, in these last few years, to *choose* the right, the godly, and the gracious attitudes toward my irregular person.

"Only You, Savior, could have done these things. But

now, today, Lord, even as I drive this freeway, I bring the inner suffering that rages as an unending fire, and I place the unhealed scars and ashes of my memories in Your healing hands. These wounds are too painful for me to keep locked up inside me anymore, and I'm so desperately worn and tired I cannot carry them a moment longer. Dear Jesus, Lord and Savior, fill me with Your life and touch me."

There was no clap of thunder, no accident with my car; nor did I miss any of the turnoffs of the five freeways I took to reach my home. But the rest of the trip was driven with a steady flow of tears and the awareness of God's healing touch.

I remember at this point I asked the Lord if He wanted me to go back over all the hurts and painful experiences I'd had over the years with my irregular person as a psychiatrist would do. And I think I almost heard a small chuckle from the Lord when He answered, "No, Joyce, it isn't necessary. I know all about every one of them."

How true, I thought. Just think of it. When we go for counseling with our Lord, we don't have to flush out the details of our hurts. It isn't necessary. He knows . . . He knows already!

The Gaither's song, "He Touched Me," poured over the havoc of my wounded memories. I knew the Lord was touching every area of my shattered emotions. He would not miss a single wound for, He lovingly reassured me, He knew those places by heart.

I felt, too, that the scars would always be there, that they would never go away. But I also knew for certain that the bleeding had stopped, and I no longer felt the crushing, piercing pain within my inner being. Also, I am old enough in the faith and know enough of God's character to understand that the healing of this day, while it was a giant one, would not be the last.

Before I reached home, I saw myself in a daytime dream

or mental vision, and that scene has never faded away. I found myself, wet and shivering with cold, standing on a sandy beach—intently watching the ocean. The strong evening tide was pulling the water out beyond the eye's ability to see. And it was as if my over forty years of emotional, stabbing pain was ebbing out of my life and going out to sea, to never return again.

I knew then, as clearly as I know my name, that my wounds had almost taken me under the sea. They had almost laid me in a watery grave, but I had survived! I was not drowning anymore, nor would I ever even come close again . . . the Lord had heard my cries and had rescued me!

Oh, dear reader, I wish I were not writing these things to you, but saying them as I sat beside you. I would hold your hand or touch your face and say, "OK, I can see how beautifully you are coping with your irregular person. Outwardly you really look and act wonderfully well. But what of those memories, what of the conscious and unconscious pictures in your mind? What of the regrets, and what of those unhealed inner scars you hide from everyone? Do you need for someone to see you, *really* see you, as my doctor saw me, so you can talk about them, admit they are there, and then open the deepest places of suffering within you to the Lord?"

I believe, with all my heart, that the Lord wanted me to share these intimate and highly personal lines with you. He wanted me to be, for you, like my doctor was for me—a person who probed, stirred your thinking, and who looked beyond your well-adjusted attitudes and ways of coping and your attempt to understand your irregular person, to your damaged inner self. I believe the Lord wanted me to help you, as I was helped.

Who, among us, does not need a cleansing or a healing of the memories? Who does not need the Lord, as a gifted surgeon, to reopen the closed wound, to clean out the hidden pus of infection, and to begin the process whereby the terrible hurts of our lives heal from the *inside out?*

Over twenty-five years ago, Agnes Sandford wrote books and taught many seminars about God's healing our invisible memories. It is still true today. And since that incredible drive on the Newport Freeway, my memories involving my irregular person have been touched by Jesus. Surprising as it was, God seemed *eager* to take my painful memories the moment I offered them up to Him. I am restored, and am emotionally whole as never before. My doctor was right, you know. He told me that only the Lord could heal these kinds of inner conflicts.

As to my jaw and head pain—they still continue. Even today, I've only been able to rewrite and work on this chapter in small increments of time. The pain has been ranging from barely tolerable to blindly acute. The same God who healed my memories can heal my body, but, for reasons known only to Him, it is not time for a physical healing. I do not know why, or have I (even today) badgered God about the "whys" of chronic pain. I only know that your system, and mine, *cannot* tolerate *combined* physical and emotional pain for long periods of time. So, for those of you who experience both types of pain, I urge you to consider laying yourself wide open before the Lord so that He can restore not merely your joy but your life.

Perhaps you and I will never be free from physical pain. Or, maybe a healing of that, too, is just around the corner, in God's plan. I don't know. But I rest easy in His compassion and timing. I wish that for you, too.

My friends, Joni Eareckson and Mary Korstjens, know God *could* take away their paralysis, but He chooses not to. Instead, He has given them an inner healing, a healing of the memories, and they are two of the most wholly complete women I know.

In the very first part of this book, I quoted the Lord's

words to Jeremiah. "Never fear their faces, for I am with you to rescue you, says the Lord" (Jer. 1:8, MLB).

We need not fear the face of our irregular person, for God is here with us, and He has promised to come and rescue us.

Watch out for the creative ways in which God heals. Never underestimate the hopelessness of the relationship which is so shattering to your soul. (After all, God used many people, including a doctor I'd never met before that summer, and gave me an inner healing on the Newport freeway when He wanted to rescue me!)

But mostly I hope you and I will see the irregular people in our lives in a proper and sane way. They must not be allowed to manipulate, control, and discourage all our efforts at walking with God and the rest of humanity.

We need to cope with our irregular person as best we can. And we need all the encouragement we can get to keep our painful hurts as infection-free as possible.

The words of the great prophet, Isaiah, have blazed across my mind for the better part of this past year. They have come to me in the best of times and in the worst of times. I've repeated these lines in the palace of well-being and in the furnace of pain. I've said them to myself in bright daylight and in the blackest part of the night. Always they have ministered to my heart, and I now pray that you will drink deeply from the cup of hope offered here:

> When you go through deep waters and great trouble, I will be with you. When you go through rivers of difficulty, you will not drown! When you walk through the fire of oppression, you will not be burned up—the flames will not consume you. For I am the Lord your God, your Savior, the Holy One of Israel (Isa. 43:2–3, TLB).

NOTES

A Letter to My Readers

1. James Brown, "Eight Is Enough's Fantasy Family," *Los Angeles Times*, 7 April 1981, p. 10.

2. Ray Stedman, *Expository Studies in Jeremiah: Death of a Nation*, A Discovery Bible Study Book (Waco, Tex.: Word Books, 1976).

Chapter One

1. Bette Green, *Summer of My German Soldier* (New York: Dial Press, 1973), screenplay by Jane Howard Hammerstein, 1978.

Chapter Two

1. From "WE REALLY DO NEED EACH OTHER," by Reuben Welch. © Copyright 1973 by Impact Books. All rights reserved. Reprinted by permission of the Benson Company, Inc., Nashville.

Chapter Three

1. Anne Ortlund, *Children Are Wet Cement* (Old Tappan, N.J.: Fleming H. Revell Co., 1980).

2. Ibid.

3. Keith Korstjens, *Not a Sometimes Love* (Waco, Tex.: Word Books, 1981).

4. Dobson, *What Wives Wish Their Husbands Knew About Women* (Wheaton, Ill.: Tyndale House Pubs., 1975), p. 183.

5. Creath Davis, *Lord, If I Ever Needed You It's Now* (Palm Springs, Calif.: Ronald H. Haynes, 1981), p. 88.

Chapter Four

1. Charles R. Swindoll, *Improving Your Serve* (Waco, Tex.: Word Books, 1981), p. 72.

Chapter Five

1. Dwight L. Carlson, *Overcoming Hurts and Anger* (Irvine, Calif.: Harvest House, 1981).

2. Ibid.

3. David Augsburger, *Caring Enough to Confront* (Glendale, Calif.: Regal Books, 1981), p. 52.

4. James Dobson, *Emotions: Can You Trust Them?* (Glendale, Calif.: Regal Books, 1980), p. 95.

Chapter Six

1. Jason Towner, *Forgiveness Is For Giving* (Nashville, Tenn.: Impact Books, Div. of The Benson Co., 1982).

Chapter Seven

1. C. S. Lewis, *Voyage of the Dawn Treader*, The Chronicles of Narnia (New York: Macmillan Publishing Co., 1952), p. 1.

RECOMMENDED FURTHER READING

Augsburger, David. *Caring Enough to Confront.* Glendale, California: Regal Books, 1981.

Carlson, Dwight L. *Overcoming Hurts and Anger.* Irvine, California: Harvest House, 1981.

Dobson, James. *Emotions: Can You Trust Them?* Glendale, California: Regal Books, 1981.

Landorf, Joyce. *Mourning Song.* Old Tappan, New Jersey: Fleming H. Revell Co., 1980.

Jacobs, Joan. *Feelings: Where They Come From and How to Handle Them.* Wheaton, Illinois: Tyndale House Pubs., 1976.

Seamands, David. *Healing of Our Damaged Emotions.* Wheaton, Illinois: Victor Books, 1981.

Solomon, Charles R. *The Ins and Outs of Rejection.* Littleton, Colorado: Heritage House Pubs., 1976.

Swindoll, Charles. *Improving Your Serve.* Waco, Texas: Word Books, 1981.

Towner, Jason. *Forgiveness Is For Giving.* Nashville, Tennessee: Impact Books, Div. of The Benson Co., 1982.

Welch, Reuben. *When You Run Out of Fantastic—Persevere.* Nashville, Tennessee: Impact Books, Div. of The Benson Co., 1976.

ABOUT THE AUTHOR

Joyce Landorf Heatherley is known nationwide as a uniquely gifted Christian communicator, able to convey biblical principles with relevance, humor, compassion and gentle conviction-- in a way that speaks to the needs of men and women from all backgrounds. A best-selling author of both fiction and non-fiction, her 24 books include: MY BLUE BLANKET, THE INHERITANCE, BALCONY PEOPLE, SILENT SEPTEMBER, MONDAY THRU SATURDAY, FRAGILE TIMES, IRREGULAR PEOPLE, HE BEGAN WITH EVE, CHANGEPOINTS, UNWORLD PEOPLE, MOURNING SONG, JOSEPH, I CAME TO LOVE YOU LATE, FRAGRANCE OF BEAUTY, RICHEST LADY IN TOWN, and her latest title, SPECIAL WORDS FOR WHEN YOU DON'T KNOW WHAT TO SAY.

Joyce is also an immensely popular speaker and conference leader. Recordings of her more popular talks, including: BALCONY PEOPLE, IRREGULAR PEOPLE, UNWORLD PEOPLE and THE INHERITANCE are available on audio cassette, as are video tapes of CHANGEPOINTS, IRREGULAR PEOPLE, and UNWORLD PEOPLE. Her HIS STUBBORN LOVE film series, based on her nationally acclaimed seminars of the same name, was the recipient of the 1981 president's award from the Christian Film Distributors Association.

Any speaking engagement requests or inquiries concerning Joyce Landorf Heatherley books, tapes and music may be directed to 1- 800-777-7949.

Visit our web site at:
www.balconypublishing.com